SOUTH

CROS

SKIING GUIDE

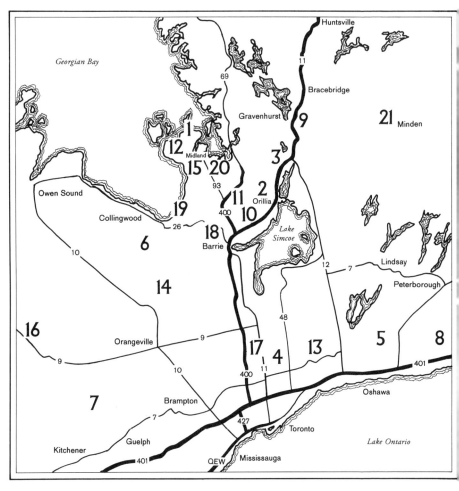

1 ... Awenda Provincial Park
2 ... Bass Lake Provincial Park
3 ... Bayview Wildwood Resort
4 ... Bruce's Mill Conservation Area
5 ... Ski Dagmar
6 ... Duntroon Highlands Nordic
7 ... Elora Gorge Conservation Area
8 ... Ganaraska Forest Centre
9 ... Gravenhurst KOA Nordic Trails
10 .. Hardwood Hills
11 ... Horseshoe Resort

12 ... Lafontaine en Action
13 ... Long Sault Conservation Area
14 ... Mansfield Outdoor Centre
15 ... Midland Mountainview
16 ... Minto Glen Winter Sports Centre
17 ... Seneca College, King Campus
18 ... Springwater Provincial Park
19 ... Wasaga Beach Provincial Park
20 .. Wye Marsh Wildlife Centre
21 ... Haliburton Highlands Lodge-to-Lodge Skiing

SOUTHERN ONTARIO
CROSS-COUNTRY
SKIING GUIDE

TERRY BURT-GERRANS

Stoddart

A BOSTON MILLS PRESS BOOK

Dedicated to the memory of my son, James, who would have
enjoyed these trails.

Canadian Cataloguing in Publication Data

Burt-Gerrans, Terry, 1941-
    Southern Ontario cross-country skiing guide

ISBN 1-55046-126-5

1. Cross-country skiing - Ontario, Southern - Guidebooks.   2. Trails -
Ontario, Southern - Guidebooks.   3. Ontario, Southern - Guidebooks.
I. Title.

GV854.8.C3B8 1994   796.93'2'09713   C94-931517-6

First published in 1994 by
Stoddart Publishing Co. Ltd.
34 Lesmill Road
Toronto, Canada
M3B 2T6
(416) 445-3333

A BOSTON MILLS PRESS BOOK
The Boston Mills Press
132 Main Street
Erin, Ontario
N0B 1T0

Illustrations and maps by Dave McWilliams
Front cover photograph courtesy of Alec Pytlowany / Masterfile
Design by Mary Firth
Printed in Canada

The publisher gratefully acknowledges the support of the Canada
Council, Ontario Ministry of Culture and Communications, Ontario
Arts Council and Ontario Publishing Centre in the development of
writing and publishing in Canada.

Contents

Introduction

This book is meant to be used as a guide to some of the popular cross-country ski areas within a reasonable driving distance of Toronto. It does not cover all of the Nordic ski areas in Southern Ontario, but it does touch on most of the areas close enough for an afternoon's skiing.

Some of the areas are commercial and some are public park or wildlife areas. Without exception, the commercial areas offer more facilities and better groomed trails. All the commercial operators, while not objecting to skiing in the park areas, suggested that new skiers would enjoy the sport more if they began by coming out to a commercial area, where they can take lessons and pick up tips on equipment and technique that will quickly make their skiing more enjoyable.

I skied each of the trails reported in this guide at some time during the 1993 and 1994 seasons. Some personal bias may show in my descriptions and in my comments on the relative difficulty of the trails. Some trails that seemed challenging in December felt quite easy after skiing every weekend all winter, especially when it came to climbing up hills. Keep in mind that trail layouts may change slightly from year to year, particularly in the less commercial areas. The times noted for each trail are times an average skier can ski it in comfortably, and may vary, depending on your skill level and whether you are after a hard workout or a pleasant ramble through the woods.

I have tried to be consistent in my descriptions of the various trails and features. For instance, if I describe a hill as a gentle climb, it means that I can climb it easily, but if it is a steep climb, I have to use the herringbone technique to get to the top. An easy downhill run is a slope I can approach and ski down without pausing, and still enjoy the view on the way down. A steep slope means that I would pause at the top to reconnoitre the track before starting down, and I would probably be too busy concentrating on the skiing to admire the scenery.

The maps used in this guide have all been drawn to a consistent format, based on maps available at each site. When planning your outing, read the detailed tours of the various trails and study the trail maps included in this guide, but always refer to the current maps provided by each ski area.

References to costs are based on 1993/94 rates. All distances from Toronto are based on a starting point at the intersection of Highways 400 and 401.

All reasonable care and diligence were used in researching the ski areas and trails in this guide, but there may be things, both good and bad, that I have overlooked. The impression you get of a ski trail depends so much on the weather and ski conditions that your opinion of a trail may vary from weekend to weekend. That's one of the things that makes cross-country skiing so interesting.

Each location has its own atmosphere and pace. Some are oriented to competitive racing skiers, some to families and novices, and some to those who use cross-country skiing to get away from crowds, jobs and the pressures of city life. The areas described here provide for all of those inclinations and more.

I hope you enjoy this book and I look forward to meeting you on the trails. Happy skiing!

The Ski Areas at a Glance

Each ski area has its own special personality that sets it apart from the other areas reported in this guide. The following thumbnail sketches of each facility show the particular attractions that make each facility unique.

Awenda Provincial Park

Awenda Provincial Park is little used in the winter and is the most remote area in this guide. It is not recommended for first-time skiers. Awenda caters to nature lovers who want the chance to be independent and to ski far from the crowds.

Bass Lake Provincial Park

Bass Lake Provincial Park is a summer camping park just outside of Orillia. In the winter you can stop by for an hour's easy skiing with the family.

Bayview Wildwood Resort

Bayview Wildwood Resort is a traditional Muskoka resort hotel that offers year-round activities. Skiing is only one of many activities available here for a day trip or for a getaway weekend.

Bruce's Mill Conservation Area

Bruce's Mill is a small park near Toronto and is one of several ski areas operated by the Metropolitan Toronto and Region Conservation Authority. It offers some very pretty trails and is an excellent place for novice skiers to get a feel for the sport.

Ski Dagmar

Ski Dagmar is a complete ski area just outside Toronto that offers cross-country and downhill skiing. All levels of cross-country trails can be found here.

Duntroon Highlands Resort

Duntroon Highlands Nordic ski area is a fairly new area located on the Niagara Escarpment just south of Collingwood. Near the highest elevation in Southern Ontario, it has more snow and a longer season than most places. The trails are well laid out and excellently groomed.

Elora Gorge Conservation Area

The conservation area at Elora Gorge offers limited skiing in a mainly flat area along a small but spectacular gorge carved out of limestone by the Grand River. This area is worth a visit for its unusual scenery, even though the skiing offers no particular challenge.

Ganaraska Forest Centre

The Ganaraska Forest Centre is part of a 4,400-hectare forest north of Port Hope. The 35 km of trails here are excellent and offer enough variety to challenge any skier. It is surprising that Ganaraska is not better known among serious skiers and wilderness lovers.

Gravenhurst KOA Nordic Trails

Gravenhurst KOA offers excellent trails through a mainly flat area of Muskoka. This area is used mainly by local people or skiers from the city who stay at winterized cottages. Winter camping is available.

Hardwood Hills

Hardwood Hills is a high-tech world-class Nordic ski facility that attracts skiers of all levels. Olympic athletes can come here to train, and strong recreational skiers can find all the challenge they desire on these trails.

Horseshoe Resort

Horseshoe Resort is a very professional resort area that offers much more than just skiing. Horseshoe is a great place for a skiing weekend. Here you can enjoy first-class Nordic or downhill skiing on excellent trails suited to all levels of experience, and have the convenience of a good hotel, restaurant and bar on the premises.

Lafontaine en Action

Lafontaine en Action is a beautiful ski area, well off the beaten path. The good trails, good service and friendly bilingual staff create an enjoyable family ski experience in a relaxed setting.

Long Sault Conservation Area

Long Sault is one of several conservation areas operated by the Central Lake Ontario Conservation Authority. It has about 17 km of very pretty trails. School groups use the trails for skiing and outdoor education every weekday during the winter.

Mansfield Outdoor Centre

Mansfield Outdoor Centre is primarily an educational area that caters to school groups during the week. Excellent, well-groomed trails are open to the public at all times. A chalet is available for group reservations on weekends.

Midland Mountainview

Mountainview is conveniently located, offers good trails, and you'll find that you are soon on a first-name basis with the friendly staff. It offers downhill as well as Nordic skiing, only a moment's drive from excellent shopping in Midland.

Minto Glen Winter Sports Centre

Minto Glen is a small, well-established ski area near Mount Forest that offers a wide range of winter activities on a small but fairly rugged forest area. This family-run, family-oriented operation, which has offered organized skiing for fifty years, provides good skiing for many local groups, as well as the general public.

Seneca College, King Campus
King Campus of Seneca College is on the old Eaton estate, home of the founder of the T. Eaton Company. The trails are well used and, considering they are only a 20-minute drive from Toronto, are quite good. Many school classes come here for ski outings each year.

Springwater Provincial Park
Springwater Provincial Park is a place to bring all the family, from tots to grandparents. The skiing and additional attractions make for an enjoyable activity-filled family outing, even if everyone doesn't ski. Many animals native to Ontario, ranging from timber wolves to porcupines, live there in a zoo setting year-round.

Wasaga Beach Provincial Park
Blueberry Plains at Wasaga Beach Provincial Park offers excellent, quiet ski trails hidden away from the honky-tonk hustle-bustle of this summer beach resort area. Wasaga could be the best-kept cross-country skiing secret in Ontario.

Wye Marsh Wildlife Centre
The Wye Marsh Wildlife Centre is an excellent family ski facility that emphasizes conservation, and the wildlife and natural history of the area.

Haliburton Highlands Lodge-to-Lodge Skiing
The Lodge-to-Lodge trail system in the Haliburton Highlands is made up of over 150 km of trails connecting eight resorts. This is not a day outing from Toronto, but a weekend or a week's vacation. It offers some unique opportunities for the intermediate or advanced skier.

Awenda Provincial Park

Awenda Provincial Park is a Natural Environment park. This means that it must comprise at least 6,000 acres (about 2,400 hectares), and that wherever possible the area must be allowed to remain in an untouched state. On the hiking and ski trails and around the camping areas, the forest environment is managed. Fallen trees and brush are cleared away in the areas used for recreation. In most of the rest of the park, intervention is kept to a minimum. The trails are well groomed, but there may be places where you will have to duck under branches from a fallen tree or step over a log lying across the path. You are not restricted to the groomed trails here. If you want to go bush-whacking and make your own route, you can go ahead. You will have a better appreciation of the stamina of the early explorers and native residents of the area who made their way through this sort of country on foot or on snowshoe.

I find Awenda a delightful place to ski. You can bring a pot of soup with you, put it on the stove at the trail centre, ski rustic, interesting trails, and return to find your soup hot and ready.

There is no ski patrol at Awenda, and no one scans the parking lot in the late afternoon to see if there are still skiers out on the trails. No searches will be initiated if your car is still sitting in the lot at 5 PM. Some people express horror when they come here and find out that they are on their own. Others come here for that very reason, for the feeling of independence that comes with being self-reliant.

Location
Awenda Provincial Park is located north of Penetanguishene, about 180 km from Toronto. Driving time from Toronto is about 2$\frac{1}{4}$ hours. Take Highway 400 north to Barrie, then take Highway 93 north to the Midland–Penetanguishene area.

Ignore all the turns into Midland and go to the third stoplight in Penetanguishene. Turn left onto Robert Street and carry on for about a kilometre, then turn right toward Lafontaine and follow the signs to Awenda Provincial Park. It seems like a long way, but don't give up. The roads are well marked. Turn right into trail centre (approximately 18 km from the centre of Penetanguishene).

Park Superintendent
Awenda Provincial Park
P.O. Box 973
Penetanguishene, Ontario
LOL 1PO
(705) 549-2231

Topography

A high hardwood plateau with a steep cliff leads down to the beach area. The forest below is cedar, balsam and hemlock in the swampy areas just back from the beach. The forest here is quite young, about forty years old over much of the area. This means that it seems quite open and airy compared to older forest areas with more mature trees.

Trail Map

The trail map at Awenda is quite adequate, but a scale on the map would help. It is often difficult to tell the length of a route, particularly the two parts of the Bluff Trail, because of the way the trails are laid out.

There are a number of You Are Here maps on the trails, and they are very helpful. Their location is marked on the trail map. There is no big trail-map board at the trail centre, and trail conditions are not posted. Trail maps are available in the warm-up hut.

Facilities

There are four trails at Awenda Provincial Park—although I tend to consider the Bluff Trail two separate trails—covering about 25 km. At the trail centre there is a good warm-up hut with a stove and firewood. Bring matches and paper just in case the fire isn't going when you get there. There are outdoor toilet facilities at the trail centre and at three other points on the trails.

Cost

The charges here are for car parking only. The cost is $6 per car per day, or $24 for a season pass to any provincial park from November 1 to March 31. As at all of the provincial parks, any number of people may ski on one parking permit.

BEACH

Length: 7 km
Time: $2^1/2$ hours
Level: Intermediate

Detailed Tour

From the parking area and warm-up hut, cross the road and turn right down the wide trail. The first part of the trail is often cut up with the footprints of people out for a short hike. It doesn't last long, and soon the trail is wide enough to ski three abreast. There is a slight downhill grade at this point, which leads to the top of a long, easy downhill run with a wide sweeping bend to the left.

Continue until you come to a fork in the trail. Take the left fork and cross the parking lot. When you are about halfway across the parking lot, turn right and go down through the trees to the beach. This downhill stretch is narrow but straight and not too steep. The trail continues through the trees along the beach to a platform lookout point.

At the side of the trail just before the lookout point, you will see a bronze plaque honouring the memory of Etienne Brûlé, an early seventeenth-century explorer believed to have been the first European to set eyes on Georgian Bay.

After stopping at the platform to admire the view across the ice, and the ice sculptures carved by the wind, take the trail up and away from the beach. This is an easy uphill ski that brings you out on the parking lot you crossed earlier.

To avoid the long uphill climb up the road, turn right at the parking lot and go along a narrow track for about 200 metres to a huge set of steps. Remove your skis and go up the steps, pausing from time to time to enjoy the view down into the forest. At the top of the steps a trail about half a kilometre long joins you to the Bluff Trail. Turn left onto the Bluff Trail and follow it to the road, then turn right for home.

Cautions

Be careful beyond the lookout platform during extremely cold weather if there is a wind from the north or northwest. The wind blowing across the trail from the open bay can cause frostbite. The return part of this trail is a long climb and can take its toll on tired leg muscles.

Variations

During good weather it is possible to ski past the lookout to near the end of Methodist Point, and even around the point on the ice. This part of the trail is not maintained, but if you like exploring it can be worthwhile. The trail is completely open to the beach for a distance of about half a kilometre, and is often windswept and almost bare of snow in places.

As you approach Methodist Point, you leave the beach for the shelter of the trees. After skiing a short distance through the trees, you come to a T-intersection. If you turn right you go back to the beach. A left turn takes you through the trees and across a narrow neck of land to the beach on the other side of the point. This far beach is so exposed to the wind that you will often find the sand beach swept clear of snow in places, even in the dead of winter. On a warm, sunny day it can be great fun for the kids to lie on the sand in ski boots and winter clothes, pretending it is summer. Other days, with a cold northwest wind blowing snow and ice particles over the frozen bay, this place can seem like a tiny bit of Antarctica.

This is the end of the trail, so turn and retrace your route to the lookout point. When the ice conditions on the bay are good for skiing, you can follow the shore to your right and around the end of Methodist Point.

The ice conditions around Methodist Point depend on temperature and wind and wave action. Sometimes it is smooth and flat and fine for skiing. At other times it is a jumble of jagged, wind-eroded ice blocks. If the ice is smooth, the route around Methodist Point can be beautiful. If it is not, don't even bother trying.

Distances across the ice can be deceiving. What looks like a short jaunt can turn into a long, cold, tiring journey. If a cold wind comes up while you are on the ice and some distance from shore, you will have no place to go for shelter. If you are skiing with the wind at your back, things can seem fine, but on a cold day that same wind can cut like a knife and freeze exposed flesh in minutes when you have to turn and face into it.

You can ski around Methodist Point in the other direction, but it is hard to find the end of the trail and the windswept beach unless you have been there a few times before.

BRÛLÉ

Length: 4 km
Time: 1 hour
Level: Novice

Detailed Tour

From the parking area and warm-up hut, go through the gate and directly onto the trails. The first part of the trail is wide and flat as it parallels the road along a slight uphill grade. At the first trail map turn right. After a short distance cross the road leading to the park office and the trail centre. Be sure to take your skis off and watch for cars when crossing the road. From here the trail winds gently through mixed hardwood bush and a summer camping ground. The going is flat and easy, but with an uphill trend. About a kilometre along, you turn right onto a road that is closed for the winter and start your way back on a slightly downhill run. After about a kilometre and a half, turn left at the sign directing you to the beaches and the trail centre. At the end of the road, skirt around the gate blocking it for the winter, and turn right again to cross the road to the trail centre.

Variations

For a slightly longer excursion, instead of turning right at the first trail map, carry on another half a kilometre and then take the Bluff Trail to the right. You can rejoin the Brûlé Trail at the road leading back to the trail centre.

BLUFF, EAST

Length: 7 km
Time: 2 hours
Level: Intermediate

Detailed Tour

From the parking lot and trail centre, go through the gate to the trails. The first section parallels the road along a wide, easy path with a slight uphill grade. At the second trail map, take the left fork to a narrower section that winds through pleasant hardwood bush. The trail here is still wide enough to ski two abreast. The young forest is open enough to admit sunlight through the trees, making this a very pretty section to ski on bright winter days.

After about a kilometre the trail narrows and begins a series of gentle slopes winding down into a narrow valley. The entire area is well sheltered from any winds. The incline becomes progressively more pronounced until you find yourself at the top of a short hill. After the first descent, the route levels off and twists easily back and forth through the trees. This is one of the most pleasant downhill runs mentioned in this book.

At the end of the descent, take the left turn up a short, steep incline. If you turn right instead of left at this point you will be starting the 5-km Wendat Trail, around Second Lake. After a short climb, the trail continues winding through the woods, giving you glimpses of Second Lake on your right. When you come to a clearing with picnic tables, toilets and a trail map, you will be halfway around the Bluff Trail. This is where the Wendat Trail rejoins the Bluff Trail.

Again take the left turn and begin the long, easy climb up to the level of the bluffs. You can go left at the summer road for a shortcut back to the trail centre, but the best of the Bluff Trail is still to come.

After about a kilometre, you cross the main road and come to the section that parallels the bluffs. At this point the ground falls away in an almost vertical drop of about 60 metres. To the north you can see Giant's Tomb Island, and farther away, to the west, Beckwith and Hope islands. Enjoy the view, but be careful to stay well back from the edge of the cliff. Along this section of the trail you will sometimes see tracks in the snow where wolves have been chasing the deer.

From here the trail continues through the woods to another trail map at a wide section that is another summer road. A left turn takes you along the road, about half a kilometre, back to the trail centre. This section of the trail is often well worn by hikers.

Variations

If you feel energetic at the bottom of the long descent in the little valley, turn right to follow the 5-km Wendat Trail around Second Lake.

When you come to the summer road back to the trail centre, you can turn right and take the long ride down the first part of the Beach Trail. Cross the parking lot and head left to return up the stairway, which joins the west half of the Bluff Trail. There, a short downhill brings you back to the trail marker where you turned off for the run down the Beach Trail hill. Half a kilometre more and you are back at the trail centre, where you can usually warm and dry yourself in front of a roaring fire.

Just after you leave Second Lake, you come to a cross trail that is a shortcut home. If you take this route home, you will find yourself on a long, wide summer road that is constantly climbing. The climb is always gentle, but it seems endless and it cuts out the best scenery of the East Bluff Trail, so I do not recommend it.

BLUFF, WEST

Length: 7 km
Time: 1 $\frac{1}{2}$ hours
Level: Intermediate

Detailed Tour

From the trail centre, go through the gate to the trails. The first stretch parallels the road along a wide, easy path, slightly uphill. At the second trail map, take the right fork onto a narrower path that winds through pleasant hardwood bush. The trail here is not wide enough to ski two abreast.

Shortly after your right turn, you meet the road into the park. Remove your skis to cross it, because the sand and road salt surely won't do the wax job on your skis any good, and it will be easier to jump if a car or snowmobile comes around the corner.

The route travels through a mixed area of young pine and hardwood forest. It is all level here with no climbing or down-hill slopes, although the general trend is upward. About 2 km after crossing the road you come to an unploughed summer road and another trail map. The shorter Brûlé Trail joins the Bluff Trail here.

Cross the summer road and continue through more hard-wood forest. You will come to some cleared areas that are the summer campgrounds, then the trail curves to the right and meanders along for another couple of kilometres before coming to a downhill section. Watch for the view across the ice to Beckwith Island, a view that is never seen from the trails in the summer when leaves are on the trees.

This area is marked on the trail map as a steep hill, but the grade is really very gentle, although narrow and winding. Partway down the slope there is another trail map where the trail from the steps up from the beach joins in. A short distance from the intersection of these two trails, you will come to the wide summer road that forms part of the Beach Trail. At the road, turn right.

The snow along this area of the trail is usually cut up from hikers and families out pulling small kids on toboggans or sleighs. Never mind that they don't ski; they are enjoying the winter outdoors in their own way!

The trail centre is only a short distance from here. Watch for cars when you cross the road into the parking area.

WENDAT

Length: 5 km
Time: 1 hour
Level: Intermediate

Detailed Tour

To reach the Wendat Trail, take the east section of the Bluff Trail from the trail centre. See the tour description for the Bluff Trail for details. This route adds at least an hour to the time required to ski the east section of the Bluff Trail. At the lowest point of the descent through the tiny valley, follow the signs and take the right turn onto the Wendat Trail. After a short ascent the trail levels off and winds through hardwood bush. On your right is a steep embankment, the remnants of an ancient shoreline when water levels here were much higher. The lake is on your left but not visible through the trees.

After about a kilometre the trail swings left and descends to the level of Second Lake. Cross the wooden causeway here over a small stream. This stream is the outlet of the lake and eventually meanders its way to Georgian Bay, so the current keeps parts of it open all winter. Don't go onto the ice.

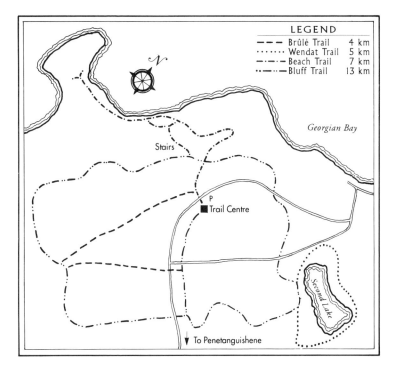

AWENDA PROVINCIAL PARK

Beyond the stream you enter a region shadowed by huge hemlock trees, an entirely different type of terrain from the hardwood forest of the first part of the trail. Skiers with any imagination at all will find this dark forest rather spooky.

About half a kilometre after entering the hemlock woods, you begin climbing and come out into a clearing where you'll find a trail map, picnic tables and toilets. Just over halfway around the lake, this makes a fine place to stop for a snack and a hot drink if you have been packing a Thermos with you. There is no warm-up hut or cooking facilities here, but on sunny days in the early spring it is a delightful place to stop and enjoy the outdoors.

The trail continues north through more hardwood forest, with the slope rising sharply on your right, allowing you good views of the lake to your left. The going is quite level, though the trail seems narrow in places. The route gradually swings away from the lake and continues through level forested area.

About 2 km past the first rest area you again approach the lake and come to another, similarly equipped rest area. This is where you rejoin the Bluff Trail. At the trail map, turn right up the hill and continue back to the trail centre.

Bass Lake Provincial Park

This small provincial park is used mainly for camping in the summer. It is closed during the winter, but many local residents use it for hiking and cross-country skiing. There are no groomed trails, and the area is small, but Bass Lake Provincial Park provides some surprisingly good skiing opportunities only a few minutes from Orillia.

It is easy to bring the kids here for an hour of skiing on a sunny afternoon. Bass Lake is also an excellent place to bring visitors from the city, even if they are not the outdoors type. You can walk or ski or just sit in the sun, without the pressure to get out and ski that is sometimes found at more formal ski areas.

Location

Bass Lake Provincial Park is located south of Highway 12, just west of Orillia. From Toronto take Highway 400 north past Barrie and turn right onto Horseshoe Valley Road. Turn right again at Highway 12, at Prices Corners, and go 2 km to Bass Lake Road, then south on Bass Lake Road for 1 km, to just past the lake. The park is on your right.

From Orillia take Highway 12 west toward Midland. Turn left onto Bass Lake Road about 2 km out of Orillia.

Topography

Bass Lake Park occupies a partly wooded hillside that slopes down to the north, to Bass Lake. There are many summer roads and campsites throughout the area. A nature trail leads east along the lakeshore, then meanders up the hill through open land to the south.

Facilities

There are no organized ski facilities or trail grooming at Bass Lake. Near the park entrance is a play area with swings and a slide and picnic tables. There are picnic pavilions with barbecue

facilities at the lakeside, less than half a kilometre from the park entrance. Bring your own charcoal for a winter picnic. The toilets are just past the picnic pavilions.

Cost

The park is closed during the winter and there appears to be no charge for use of the park in the off season.

MAIN LOOP

Length: 3 km
Time: $^1\!/_2$ hour
Level: Novice

Detailed Tour

From the parking area, follow the line of the lakeshore, past the picnic and swimming areas. When you come to a fork, take the right-hand trail, beside the lake, passing several picnic pavilions.

About half a kilometre from the parking area, past the toilets, you will set out on the nature trail, which follows a boardwalk through a low swampy area of tangled cedar woods. Although very short, it is a surprisingly pleasant section, with lots of birds, especially chickadees.

After leaving the cedar woods you come to the park boundary. Turn left and go up the hill. The sketch at the beginning of this chapter shows a narrow lane of freshly planted trees. The route goes up to the left from the point shown in the sketch. The trail then enters an area of open fields scattered with small bushes and trees, continuing up a gentle grade, and eventually swings right, then left, and starts down the hill.

The descent is an easy, shallow grade that follows the summer road and eventually rejoins your outward track. The parking area is a short distance straight ahead.

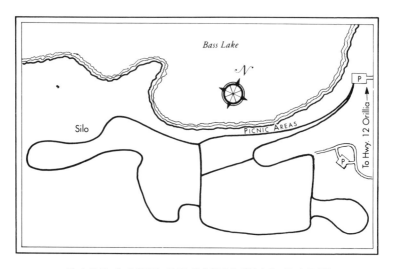

BASS LAKE PROVINCIAL PARK

Variations

You could take one of two branches that cut to the left on the long uphill grade across the open area. These lead back down to the beach and picnic pavilion area.

Bayview Wildwood Resort

The Bayview Wildwood Vacation and Conference Resort is an all-season family resort that provides good cross-country skiing along with a number of other winter activities perfect for a getaway weekend. The skiing is not the main attraction at Bayview Wildwood, since the most difficult trails here will not hold the interest of the expert skier for long. During school breaks you will find many families here taking advantage of the varied facilities; in January and February there are more couples than families.

Location

Bayview Wildwood is located about 20 km north and west of Orillia. The distance from Toronto is about 130 km; driving time is just under 2 hours. Take highway 400 north to Barrie, then Highway 11 past Orillia. About 12 km north of Orillia turn right onto the South Sparrow Lake Road. Keep following the South Sparrow Lake signs, turning right until you go over the highway, then turn left at the T-junction. A sign at the intersection points to Bayview Wildwood, 8 km away. Soon after you cross the railway tracks you are there.

Bayview Wildwood Resort
RR 1
Severn Bridge, Ontario
P0E 1N0
(705) 526-2338

Topography

Bayview Wildwood faces Sparrow Lake to the north. The entire area is covered with young mixed hardwood and pine forest. Southwest of the resort, a shallow ridge of granite crosses the area. The ski trails cross over to some small lakes on the far side of the ridge.

Trail Map

The trail map here is excellent, although not to scale. Trails are clearly colour-coded with ribbons tied to the trees—red for advanced, blue for intermediate, and yellow for novice trails.

Facilities

Bayview Wildwood resort offers much more than skiing. Besides ski and snowshoe rentals, snowmobiles are available, as are guided snowmobile safaris. An ice-skating rink is cleared on the lake, and horsedrawn sleigh rides and occasional broomball games are organized.

The resort accommodates up to 150 people. Restaurant and bar facilities are, of course, available. You'll also find all the usual resort amenities, including a swimming pool and sauna, squash courts, billiards and table tennis. There is a program of indoor and outdoor activities for children ages five to twelve.

Cost

The cost varies from $6 to $12 for daily use of the ski trails. Three-day weekend packages for the entire resort facilities vary from $116 to $150 per person.

BEAVER LAKE LOOP

Length: 4 km
Time: 50 minutes
Level: Intermediate

Detailed Tour

From the parking lot at the resort, walk past the laundry facilities and cross the railroad track. Trains run frequently along this main CNR cross-country line. Just past the tracks, cross the road to the start of the trail area. This is all ploughed, so you should carry your skis until you cross the road.

Now you are at the start of the Beaver Lake Loop. Follow the signs to the right, past the ball diamond. Soon the Trestle

Marsh Trail branches to the right. Keep left here for the Beaver Lake Loop. The first part of the loop circles an open field on top of a dike around a pond. This is quite short, but it is open to the wind. Skiers who are not properly dressed for the weather should be careful here on cold, windy days. After circling the field, novices can continue back to the ball diamond and home. There is always hot chocolate waiting at the ski shop in the resort.

The Beaver Lake Loop starts with a short, fairly steep climb into the woods. This is young, mixed hardwood forest with some pines. The way is narrow and winds through scenic woods, mostly climbing gently. After a shortcut marked for intermediate skiers branches off to the left, the trail climbs easily to a small pine meadow at the top of the ridge. Another short-cut branches off to the left here.

The trail then snakes down the far side of the ridge in a short, very narrow descent. After the downhill section, the going is mostly level until you approach Beaver Lake on your right. From this very small lake you begin a series of gentle climbs back up the ridge to arrive back at the pine meadow. The descent down this side of the ridge is a pleasant series of easy drops through trees and large granite outcroppings.

The intermediate shortcut rejoins the trail just before the final descent, the only open straight run on the trail, to the field and the ball diamond. Take your skis off at the road for the short walk back to the resort.

TRESTLE MARSH LOOP

Length: 7 km
Time: 1 ½ hours
Level: Intermediate

Detailed Tour

The beginning of the Trestle Trail is the same as the Beaver Lake Loop. From the parking lot at the resort, walk past the laundry and cross the railroad track. This is a main CNR cross-

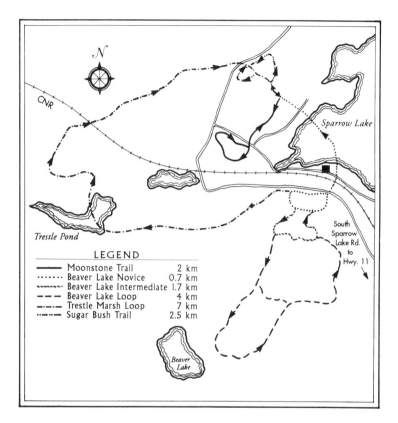

BAYVIEW WILDWOOD RESORT

country line, so watch out for frequent trains. Carry your skis until you have crossed the road past the tracks to the start of the trail.

Follow the signs to the right, past the ball diamond. Soon there is a branching to the right, where the Trestle Marsh Trail begins.

The trail starts with a quick, flat ski through open woods and joins the road for a short distance, then turns left and climbs into a forest of mostly young hardwood, with some pines. The route winds back and forth, always narrow and very pleasant. It skirts the edge of a large beaver pond and then climbs gently up the granite ridge.

Near the top of the ridge you cross a snowmobile trail that leads to Long Lake. An interesting downhill section curls down to pass a sheer granite cliffside. Melting snow sometimes spills over the edge of the cliff to form a series of spectacular frozen waterfalls.

Descend to the level of Trestle Pond and cross the pond where the trail route is well marked with stakes in the ice. The trail then zigzags and crosses another marshy pond area and begins a climb to the summit of the second ridge. At the top you may see the tracks of others who have skied off to the right to get a fine view of the marsh you just crossed. The path then winds through open forest, generally following the top of the ridge, until it nears the railroad track. Parts of this area are open and can be very exposed if the wind is blowing hard.

Once across the track the trail drops steeply for a short distance and runs along the bottom of a tiny valley with granite outcroppings on both sides. This area is all open hardwood forest. Judging from the number of tracks, there is a sizable deer population in this little valley. Just when you are beginning to wonder where this is leading, you come to a road.

Cross the road and go past the toboggan run, approaching a flat marsh area. Just before the marsh there is a branch to the left. This is the Sugar Bush Loop, a short trail that circles around a small hill, climbing gently. Where the loop rejoins the main Trestle Trail Loop there is a very short, steep descent with no room to turn at the bottom. It is best to sidestep down this part and retrace your way past the toboggan hill.

From here the trail crosses first the marsh and then the lake for the final short run to the resort. The run crossing the open lake can be very cold at times. The trail ends at the skating rink, right in front of the ski shop, where there is an endless supply of hot chocolate.

Variations

Near the end of the marsh, just before you start across the lake to the resort, the short Moonstone Trail branches right. This route crosses the marsh and loops through a flat section of forest, passing the barn for the horses used for sleigh rides.

Bruce's Mill
Conservation Area

Bruce's Mill is a small conservation area just outside Toronto. It has some pretty trails and is very popular, particularly with novice skiers who don't want to make an all-day expedition to go skiing. This is a place for families, where it is not unusual to see small kids watching the scenery pass by from the comfort of their dad's backpack.

This is one of five ski areas operated by the Metropolitan Toronto and Region Conservation Authority; all offer well-run and economical skiing on short, simple runs.

Location
Bruce's Mill is located just off Highway 404 near Stouffville. The distance from Toronto is about 30 km and you can easily drive it in less than half an hour. From the Highway 401–Don Valley Parkway area, take Highway 404 and exit right on the Stouffville Road. The area is on your right about 3 km from the highway.

The Metropolitan Toronto and Region Conservation
    Authority
5 Shoreham Drive
Downsview, Ontario
M3N 1S4
(416) 661-6600

Topography
The site is fairly flat and is divided by Bruce Creek, a small stream forming a shallow ravine that cuts through the entire area. Bruce Creek is part of the headwaters of the Rouge River. The area is mostly wooded, with reforested pine and some young hardwood forest. Part of the trail crosses an area of open meadow.

Trail Map

The trail map here is excellent. It is always easy to pinpoint your location and see how far you have to go to get back to the chalet.

Facilities

There is an excellent chalet at the ski centre, with tables for bring-your-own picnic lunches and clean washrooms. A wide choice of ski rentals is available. There are no toilets on the trails and no facilities for heating your own food.

Cost

A day ski pass here is $7 for adults and $3 for children.

ALL

Length: 5 km
Time: $1\frac{1}{4}$ hours
Level: Novice to intermediate

Detailed Tour

This is a single loop trail with two shortcuts. The main 5-km trail is the Red Trail. There are two shortcuts that reduce the length of the run. The first, the Green Trail, reduces the route to a short, easy 1.3 km. The second, the intermediate Blue Trail, covers the main part of the route but is only 4 km long.

From the chalet, cross a short open area to the woods. The first part of the trail is all flat and easy. It stays just inside the edge of the woods, beside the road. After a bit more than half a kilometre, the Green Trail branches off to your left, where it cuts through some pine forest before rejoining the main trail.

After the Green Trail junction, the main Red Trail drops down and crosses a small stream, then ascends in a short, steep climb back to the level of the main road. This section is very pretty, with reforested pine on your right and some old hardwoods on the left.

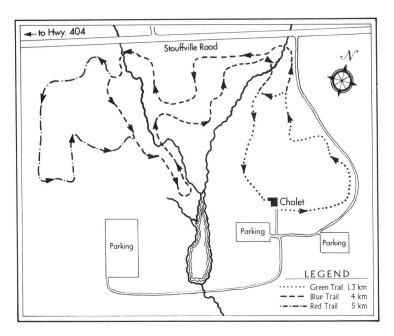

BRUCE'S MILL CONSERVATION AREA

The trail loops around some private property and drops down to cross Bruce Creek, then climbs back out of the ravine to an open area. To take the Blue Trail, follow the branch to the left beside the woods. If you want more exercise, turn right and ski the 1-km loop around the edge of the open area. (This is all exposed and can be very cold at times.)

After you rejoin the Blue Trail, the rest of the way is through mixed forest. Soon after you enter the forest you come to a nice downhill section that heads left, then loops around and follows the creek along the ravine bottom for a bit before crossing a bridge and climbing up into the woods again. After one more fairly steep downhill run, ending with a right turn, you rejoin the Green Trail for a short, pleasant ski through the forest and a final, easy climb to the chalet.

Ski Dagmar

Ski Dagmar is a complete ski resort. Although the emphasis is on downhill skiing and snowboarding, Dagmar offers 25 km of well-maintained cross-country trails, providing a variety of challenges to appeal to all levels of skiers.

School groups are welcomed and there is a special area groomed for teaching cross-country skiing. There is even snow-making equipment for the maintenance of the cross-country ski trails.

Location

Ski Dagmar is located about 20 km north of Ajax, about 35 km from Toronto, and it takes about 40 minutes from the intersection of Highways 400 and 401. Take Highway 401 east and exit north on Harwood Avenue at Ajax. Turn right onto Highway 2 and travel 5 km to Lakeridge Road. Turn left onto Lakeridge. Ski Dagmar is on your left, about 15 km north.

Ski Dagmar
RR 1
1220 Lakeridge Road
Ashburn, Ontario
L0B 1A0
(905) 649-2002

Topography

Ski Dagmar lies in a shallow valley. The alpine ski area is on the south side and the cross-country trails snake through the forested north slope of the valley. Several small ravines cut through the cross-country area.

Trail Map

The trail map is adequate, although better signs on the trails would be a help.

Facilities

Cross-country facilities here include a snack bar in the chalet, and a waxing room, but waxing irons are not available. There are over a thousand pairs of rental skis available. In the main chalet at the alpine ski area there is a bigger snack bar and a luncheon area where you can sit and watch the downhill skiers on the slopes. There are rest rooms at the chalet but no toilet facilities on the trails.

Cost

Trail fees are $10 per day on weekends and $8 per day during the week. Seniors and students pay $8 per day.

Special Features

I have been told that the Jackrabbit Trail was laid out by the famous ski racer Jackrabbit Johannsen. I can't verify the truth of this, but it is a very interesting trail, with enough steep slopes, both up and down, to give any skier a good workout.

DEER

Length: 4.75 km
Time: 1 hour
Level: Intermediate

Detailed Tour

From the chalet, follow the express trail past the snow-making pond. The route here is very wide and open. On your left is the gentle slope groomed for teaching cross-country techniques to novices. As you enter the forest the trail narrows but is still quite wide and groomed for two-way traffic. To ski only the Deer Trail, keep to the right where the Pine Valley Loop branches off. The trail descends here in a shallow slope to the Meeting Place, an open area at the far end of the trail.

A short, steep climb takes you up to the Resting Place. From here you can see the Meeting Place, so it makes a fine area to wait and watch if you have arranged to meet someone there.

After you leave the Resting Place you come to an easy downhill run to a major trail junction. Continue left, up the hill, then branch off to the left, but be sure that you don't take the far left path, where the end of the Jackrabbit Trail joins the main trails for the run home.

The Deer Trail climbs fairly steeply to a wide open area, then passes a huge pine tree and comes to a fairly steep downhill slope. This slope angles right near the bottom and is often quite rough. Then it doubles back to the right and climbs back up, parallel to the road.

Once you are back at the top the going is open and easy, mostly a very gentle descent, past the junction with the Jackrabbit Trail. Keep to the left at the bottom and join the main two-way trail back to the chalet. The gentle downhill section just before the chalet is quite open and can feel very exposed in frostbite weather.

HILLTOP LOOP

Length: 1.5 km
Time: $^1/_2$ hour
Level: Intermediate

Detailed Tour

From the chalet, follow the directions on the trail map and turn left at the main trail-map board. Take the main trail around the side of the hill until you can see the alpine chalet. The Hilltop Loop turns right here and goes straight up the hill. At the top you will find an excellent view of the entire alpine area.

The trail then enters hardwood forest, where it follows the edge of a ravine for a short distance but never drops down into the ravine. After a very short loop it comes out into the open near the lookout area.

The trail ends with a moderately steep downhill run to the teaching hill. This is not a difficult slope, but the area has so much traffic that the snow is often cut up and rutted, making the footing difficult. At the end of the loop you can return to the chalet or continue straight on to the Pine Valley, Jackrabbit and Deer trails.

PINE VALLEY

Length: 3 km
Time: $^3/_4$ hour
Level: Novice

Detailed Tour

The Pine Valley Trail is a short, easy, loop trail. It can be used as a variation of the Jackrabbit and Deer trails to add distance to the expedition. This trail is well used by school groups and beginners, so the tracks are often cut up and rough.

From the chalet follow the signs for the main trails around the snowmaking pond. Shortly after you pass the teaching hill, the Pine Valley Trail turns left, starting with a shallow downhill ski into the pine woods.

At the far point of the loop there is a slight downhill that is often cut up with body-sized craters. Here the trail reverses and begins an equally slight uphill climb straight through the forest to the end of the loop.

The Pine Valley Trail rejoins the main loop near where it started. From here you can go on to the Deer or Jackrabbit trails or back to the chalet. The last part of the main trail is quite open and can be very cold if there is a wind blowing, so watch out for frostbite in extreme conditions.

JACKRABBIT

Length: 7.5 km (via Pine Valley Trail)
Time: $1^3/_4$ hours
Level: Expert

Detailed Tour

To get to the start of the Jackrabbit Trail, follow the Deer Trail to the Meeting Place, an open area at the far end of the Pine Trail. See the Deer Trail tour for a description of this section.

From the Meeting Place, take the branch to the left, up a short, steep climb to the top of the hill, where there is a bench to rest on. The trail becomes narrow here and climbs gently along the side of a ridge, then drops fairly steeply down. The descent is followed by a sharp turn to the right and the start of a long, steep climb back up the ridge. Partway up, a shortcut branches right, cutting off a lot of the Jackrabbit Trail.

Beyond the shortcut the climb is much gentler and eventually comes to a lookout point. From the lookout it is not far to a very steep but short and straight downhill. The forest here is all hardwood, with open fields on your left. After the downhill the trail again climbs, this time to the highest point on the run, and turns to the right, following the edge of the forest. In times of extreme cold with a strong wind blowing from the north, this section can be quite exposed and drifted.

Now comes the reward for all your climbing—a series of twisting descents with only a few short climbs through scenic forest. There are some interesting turns on this section, so be careful not to let your speed build up too much unless you can clearly see the trail ahead of you.

After a final downhill you come to the rest area you passed at the start of the trail. If you go straight ahead you come to the Meeting Place. To ski the rest of the Jackrabbit Trail, keep to the left, up the hill. This section is again mostly up and down, but much less rugged and with fewer sharp turns than the first section.

When you come to a high, open area, you will see the road and the Deer Trail on your left. Shortly after that you ride a short, steep downhill with a very sharp left turn near the top. A snow fence has been set up on the outside of the turn here to stop you from going over the edge.

A final climb brings you to an easy downhill run, where you merge with two-way traffic on the Deer Trail. If you are returning to the chalet, turn right here, across the traffic coming up the hill, and enjoy the fast run down to the main trail back to the chalet. In extreme conditions take precautions against frostbite on this last part of the trail.

WEST TRAILS
(EVERGREEN ALLEY AND MEADOWVIEW)

Length: 2.5–3 km
Time: ¾ hour
Level: Novice

Both of these trails are quite open and essentially flat. They are for the most inexperienced novice skiers and have very little to recommend them. Even if you have never skied before, you would probably have a better time on the Pine Valley Trail than on either of these trails.

Detailed Tour
Follow the main trail around the side of the hill past the alpine chalet. This is all a two-way traffic area. Once past the chalet you come to an open field.

The Evergreen Alley Trail goes straight ahead up a slight hill and across the field. Then it enters a dense pine forest for a short distance, makes a tiny loop and comes out into the open again, where it crosses another part of the field and joins up with the Meadowview Trail.

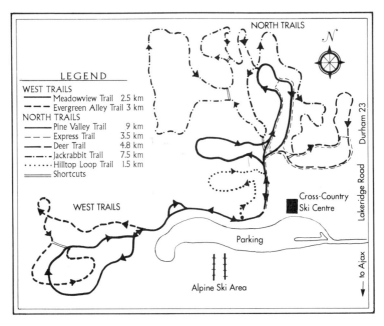

SKI DAGMAR

The Meadowview Trail circles around the edge of the open field, climbing a slight incline and then dropping back down after it is joined by the Evergreen Alley Trail. The trails loop around the field, then run back past the alpine chalet to the cross-country chalet.

Duntroon Highlands Nordic

The Highlands Nordic ski area, operated at Duntroon Highlands Resort, is a very professional ski facility that offers 15 km of excellent, well-kept trails. Family skiing is encouraged here. You can even rent a pulka, or baby glider, for pulling infants on the trails. Since the area is near the point of highest elevation in Southern Ontario, it has the best climate conditions for snow and therefore the longest ski season within easy driving distance of Toronto.

The trails were designed by experienced skiers to provide enjoyable skiing for the largest possible number of skiers. While there is a good variety of elevation, there are no trails here beyond the ability of a good intermediate skier.

Location

Highlands Nordic is located just west of Stayner and south of Collingwood. The distance from Toronto is about 140 km; driving time is 1½ hours. Follow Highway 400 north to Barrie and then Highway 26 west to Stayner. Go straight through Stayner onto Highway 91 to Duntroon. As you approach Duntroon you will see the road ahead rising up the Niagara Escarpment. About 3 km past Duntroon turn left at the sign. The ski area is about 2 km after the turn. The drive into the resort is quite steep; don't worry, it's not as bad as it looks, and very few cars are stranded there until spring.

An alternate route is to take Airport Road directly north to Stayner and then turn left to Duntroon.

Highlands Nordic Inc.
P.O. Box 110
Duntroon, Ontario
L0M 1H0
(705) 444-5017

Topography

Highlands Nordic is located on the top of the Niagara Escarpment. The area is covered in mature upland hardwood forest, with a few patches of evergreen woods. The trails take full advantage of the varied terrain. The chalet is located at an elevation of about 420 metres above sea level, and the highest point of the trails is at almost 540 metres, which makes for some good downhill runs back to the trail centre.

There are some fine views to the northeast. You can see to Stayner and Collingwood, and across the southern part of Georgian Bay to Midland and beyond.

Trail Map

The trail map looks a bit light on detail at first, but you will have no difficulty in determining exactly where you are. There are good markers on the trails to indicate the route, but no distance indicators have been posted, so as to intrude as little as possible on the natural beauty of the area.

Facilities

Facilities here are excellent. A full range of equipment is available for rent, including "short skis" and racing poles for skating. There is a good waxing room with irons, and a complete line of waxes is available. There is also a very impressive-looking toboggan hill. There are washrooms at the chalet but not on the trails.

Ski lessons are available for individuals or groups. Book your lessons at least 24 hours in advance. The ski trails are patrolled by the ski patrol on weekends.

A fully licensed restaurant at the chalet offers a good lunch. When I asked what makes this ski area unique, I was told that there is a local brew, Creemore Springs beer, on tap. You can find accommodation at the Highlands Nordic Farmhouse right next door. The Farmhouse is open year-round and offers golf and hiking on the Bruce Trail in the summer.

Cost

An adult trail pass costs $9 on weekends and $7 on week-days. Special ski and meal packages are available for groups.

ORANGE
(WITH RED EXTENSION AND YELLOW VARIATION)

Length: 6.3 km (10 km with Red extension)
Time: $1^3/_4$ hours ($2^1/_2$ hours on Red extension)
Level: Expert

Detailed Tour

All trails depart the chalet from the door of the waxing room. The first, short part of the trails, which crosses the bottom of the toboggan hill, is exposed in cold, windy weather.

Once beyond the open section you enter the forest and begin climbing the escarpment through mature, open hardwood forest. The trail is groomed with a single set track down one side and a wide skating area. Even though it climbs a long way, the ascent is not steep or difficult. It is broken up into a series of stages that loop back and forth across the hill, with some easy downhill runs. The short Yellow Trail follows the same route up the hill, but uses a series of cutoffs to eliminate many of the longer loops.

Once at the top of the hill, the trail meanders through very pleasant forest with some interesting up and down sections, including one fast, straight downhill that is a lot of fun. Soon after the Red Trail branches off, the Orange Trail brings you to the beginning of the descent back to the chalet. There is a fine view of the surrounding countryside, Georgian Bay, and, in clear weather, as far as Midland, about 50 km away.

The descent from here is made in two easy stages. It is mostly open and exposed to the wind, so watch out for frostbite in very cold weather. The first part of the descent is not steep and goes straight down the face of the hill, to where the Red and Blue trails meet you. A short, level stretch crosses the hill, then you ride the last downhill to the flat area approaching the chalet.

RED EXTENSION

The Red Trail adds about 4 km to the Orange Trail, mostly through terrain similar to parts of the Orange Trail on the top of the hill. One part of this trail, about three-quarters of a kilometre long, is very open and exposed to all winds.

BLUE

Length: 2 km
Time: ¹/₂ hour
Level: Intermediate

Detailed Tour

The Blue Trail runs with the Orange Trail across the bottom of the toboggan hill. Once you have crossed the open section, you enter the forest and begin climbing the escarpment. Soon the Blue Trail branches left and begins a fairly steep climb up the side of the hill. At the top it levels out and crosses the crest of the toboggan hill. There is a good view across the southern part of Georgian Bay from here.

From here you come to a junction with the Orange and Red trails. The Blue Trail runs across the open side of the hill for a short distance and then loops back to where the other trails begin the final descent to the chalet.

This trail is quite short and open and is within sight of the chalet for most of the way. Think of the Blue Trail as an easy route to the top of the final downhill run, but not as pretty or interesting as some other trails.

GREEN

Length: 2.5 km
Time: ³/₄ hour
Level: Novice

Detailed Tour

The Green Trail also crosses the bottom of the toboggan hill, but it has a slightly different start from the other trails. Watch for the signs.

Once past the toboggan hill and into the forest, the Green Trail begins a long, gentle climb up the side of the hill through young, open hardwood forest. This is an easy climb, but it is more than some novices may be used to, and so provides a good chance to try something more challenging than the usual, very flat novice trails.

Partway up the hill a shortcut branches off to your right, and takes you down a gentle, curving slope, into an open area with cedar trees and a beaver pond. Just beyond the pond you rejoin the main trail.

If you don't take the shortcut, continue uphill, still an easy climb. Just when you can see the hill rising steeply on your left, and are wondering if you can make it, you find you have reached the top of this trail. Here the trail turns sharply to the right and begins the long, rewarding run down.

After a short uphill climb, you soon break out of the forest. Cross the creek and then tackle the short but moderately steep climb out of the tiny valley. Once out in the open again, beware the cold winds sweeping down from the escarpment. There should be no problem on this last section of trail as long as you are properly dressed for the weather conditions.

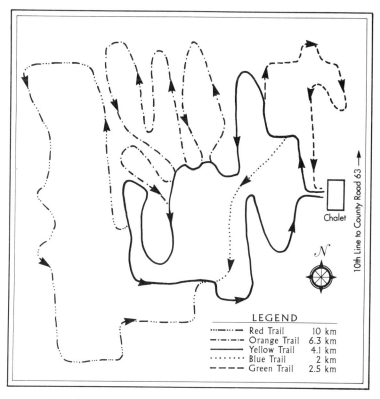

LEGEND

·········	Red Trail	10 km
─··─··─	Orange Trail	6.3 km
────────	Yellow Trail	4.1 km
··········	Blue Trail	2 km
─ ─ ─ ─	Green Trail	2.5 km

DUNTROON HIGHLANDS NORDIC

Elora Gorge
Conservation Area

The Elora Gorge is a small, steep-sided canyon that has been eroded into the limestone rock of the Niagara Escarpment. The gorge was formed by the same processes that formed Niagara Falls. A quarter of a million people visit the area each year, mostly in the summer, for camping and picnicking. The conservation area has about 10 km of groomed ski trails.

Location

Elora Gorge Conservation Area is a small park on the Grand River near the town of Elora, about 30 km north of Guelph. From Toronto take Highway 401 west and exit north on Highway 6 to Guelph. Follow the signs carefully about 15 km from the 401, as Highway 6 turns right and then left a few blocks later. At the town of Marden watch for the left turn onto County Road 7 to Elora. At Elora turn left at the flashing light; the ski area is on your right about a kilometre from the light. Driving time is about $1^{1}/_{4}$ hours from Toronto; the distance is about 110 km.

Elora Gorge Conservation Area
Grand River Conservation Authority
P.O. Box 356
Elora, Ontario
N0B 1S0
(519) 846-9742

Topography

The land surrounding Elora Gorge is mainly flat, so the skiing here is all level, except when the trails dip into the gorge itself, which is over 20 metres deep. There are many signs warning you to keep back from the edge.

Trail Map

The trail map is excellent and shows enough topographical detail that you can orient yourself from almost anywhere on the trails. There is a large trail map where the trails start.

Facilities

Facilities are limited. There are skis for rent, but be sure to call ahead to make arrangements. To get to the parking lot and the start of the trails, turn right just after the gatehouse and follow the road for a few hundred metres to past the picnic pavilion.

Cost

The cost to ski is $4.50 per person for the day. When park attendants are busy the office door may be locked, and a notice will advise you to use the honour system and deposit your trail fees in a box at the gate.

Special Features

The town of Elora has been called the most beautiful village in Ontario. The main part of the town is nestled in a valley at the head of the gorge. Many of the old buildings have been preserved and converted into inns, restaurants, gift shops and boutiques. Everyone I met there was very friendly, even going out of their way on a bitterly cold day to walk up the street with me to make sure I wouldn't get lost.

GREEN

Length: 3.5 km
Time: $^3/_4$ hour
Level: Novice

Detailed Tour

The trails start at the big trail map in the parking lot. The first part of the trail passes through an area of open cedar woods and picnic areas. After about a kilometre of easy going, turn to your right and cross the park roadway to the sports field. This section is fairly short but is quite open and barren and can be cold if there is a strong wind blowing. The trail circles the sports field and eventually crosses the road again, where it enters dense cedar woods and becomes much more scenic. The odd clearing in the woods is a summer picnic area.

Near the end of the trail you approach the gorge itself. There is a slight downhill slope here, made more interesting by the railings that suddenly appear on your right. Your reaction to your first glimpse of the gorge will probably be one of awe. The gorge really is deep!

The edges are sheer, just like the side of a building. There are railings along the edge of the walkway wherever it approaches the lip of the gorge. It should be an unnecessary warning, but don't go beyond the railings—people have died from falling over the edge.

The trail follows a walkway along the edge of the gorge for a short distance. A bridge leading across the gorge provides a spectacular view of the river below, giving you some idea of the power of the water that has carved this gorge out of solid limestone over the past 12,000 years.

From the bridge there is only a short uphill climb through more cedar forest to the parking lot.

RED (WITH BLUE VARIATION)

Length: 3.9 km
Time: 1 hour
Level: Intermediate

Detailed Tour

The Red Trail provides the most interesting skiing at Elora. From the big trail map follow the Red Trail markers past the picnic pavilion. For most of the way you will be in

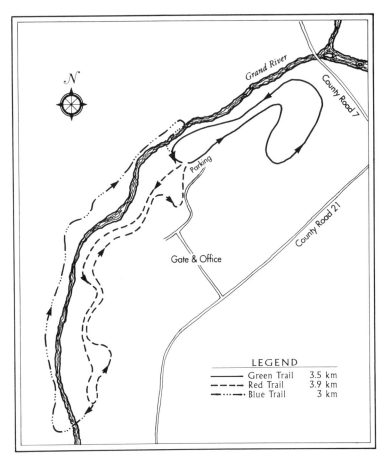

ELORA GORGE CONSERVATION AREA

cedar woods and camping areas. Part of the route follows the
road past the swimming area, a dammed-up part of a stream.

Once past the swimming hole you enter more cedar forest
and approach the edge of the gorge. There are no guardrails
here, so be very careful. This is the loveliest part of all the trails
at Elora. The way drops down slightly, with a few narrow turns
on the downhill sections.

After the trail leaves the edge of the gorge, it climbs through
open cedar woods back to the level of the roadway. Beyond the

shelter of the trees you come to the beginning of the Blue Trail. The Red Trail circles to the left and retraces the route back to the picnic pavilion. The return journey is much easier.

BLUE TRAIL VARIATION

Instead of following the Red Trail on the return trip, turn right onto the Blue Trail when you come out of the woods. This trail crosses the river and follows the west side of the gorge, which is mostly flat and exposed, and not very pretty as it goes through open camping areas. But at the end it enters the cedar woods again and comes right to the lip of the gorge. You get the best views of the gorge from this trail, so it is worth putting up with the boring part.

The trees are not too thick at the edge, so you get a fine view both upstream and downstream. Even in the coldest weather the river is open here as it tumbles over the rocks. Springs in the rock face create spectacular frozen waterfalls as high as the walls of the gorge.

At the end of this trail you come to a roadway that goes partway down into the gorge. The trail is wide and easy to ski, but at the bottom there is a left turn onto the bridge across the gorge. This bridge is also part of the end of the Green Trail. After the bridge it is a short climb through the woods to the parking lot.

Ganaraska Forest Centre

The Ganaraska Forest Centre, part of a 4,200-hectare (10,400-acre) forest, is an example of a successful conservation project. Over forty percent of the area has been replanted, resulting in a return from a sandy wasteland to a living, vibrant forest. The forest is used year-round for many activities, including skiing, hiking, horseback riding, and snowmobiling.

In the winter the central forest area is reserved for cross-country skiing. The emphasis here is on family skiing. The 35 km of narrow and winding groomed trails travel through reforested pine and spruce and both young and mature hardwood areas. The trails are maintained regularly, but are not manicured into broad highways through the woods. This is cross-country skiing with the accent on country.

Location

The Ganaraska Forest is located east of Oshawa, just north of Highway 401. It is about 110 km from Toronto and the driving time is about $1^1/_4$ hours.

Take the 401 east and exit north onto Highways 35/115 to Kirby, about 10 km away. At Kirby turn right onto Ganaraska 9 (also known as County Road 9). About 9 km from Kirby turn left at the sign for Ganaraska Forest. The centre is only about 5 km from this turn, just past the No Exit sign.

Ganaraska Region Conservation Authority
P.O. Box 328
Port Hope, Ontario
L1A 3W4
(905) 885-8173

Topography

The Ganaraska Forest is located on top of the Oak Ridge Moraine. The moraine, formed by the action of two glaciers, is one of the most significant features of the Southern Ontario landscape. It is over 160 km long, stretching from the Niagara Escarpment to the Trent River, and is characterized by jumbled, steep, forest-covered hills. Every effort is being made to restore the forest cover where it has been stripped away, exposing the soil to wind and rain erosion. The result is a diverse mix of forest types over steep hills, deep ravines, and small plateaus.

Trail Map

The trail map here is quite detailed, and looks a bit confusing at first because summer roads and a couple of snowmobile trails that cross the area are also shown. Once you learn to look just at the ski trails the map becomes much clearer. The distances shown on the map often do not agree with the distances stated by staff at the Forest Centre, but I have quoted round-trip distances that seem reasonable considering the time it took me to ski them.

From the trail centre there are two ways to get onto all the trails. The advanced route goes straight up the side of a fairly steep hill, pauses at the top, and then drops almost as steeply down the other side, with a slight turn partway down. The intermediate route circles around and joins the advanced portion near the bottom of the hill. If you doubt your ability, take the intermediate route, at least the first time you ski here.

Facilities

The facilities here are limited. There is a large chalet—actually a gymnasium complete with basketball nets. However, it is warm, and on weekends a small snack bar is set up with sandwiches and hot dogs. There are toilets at the chalet. There are no ski rentals available.

Cost

The cost is $6 per person for a day pass. For $50 you can purchase a membership in the Ganaraska Forest, which gives a family unlimited use of the ski facilities for a season.

Special Features

The Ganaraska Forest Centre is a popular site for school activities, including overnight camping. During the winter the main activity is skiing; in the spring there are sugar bush activities, and in the summer there is hiking and biking on the trails.

BLUE

Length: 5.7 km
Time: 1 $^1/_2$ hours
Level: Intermediate

Detailed Tour

The very pleasant Blue Trail, like all of the trails here, starts out with two variations—a climb over a steep hill and down the other side, or a level trail around the hill. Take your choice!

The first part of the trail mounts steadily into the forest with the Orange Trail. After you drop down into the reforested area, the Blue Trail branches off to the right, then climbs up again into a region of mixed hardwood forest. Like all the trails at Ganaraska, it continues to twist and wind through the woods, never straight and level, and always interesting.

None of the hills on the Blue Trail is particularly steep or difficult. This is a good trail to try if you are a novice skier ready to take on the challenge of a slightly longer and more difficult route. For the expert skier, this is a fine trail to ski as a warm-up before lunch, or to complete the day after skiing the Orange Trail in the morning.

Near the end of this trail, join the Yellow Trail for the final descent to the trail centre.

YELLOW

Length: 4.3 km
Time: 1 hour
Level: Intermediate

Detailed Tour

The Yellow Trail at Ganaraska Forest is the shortest trail here and can be enjoyed by skiers of any ability, although novices will find it a considerable challenge. From the trail centre, choose either the advanced or intermediate route to the trails. Once the two routes join, you are faced with a long but not too steep climb. After about half a kilometre, the Yellow Trail branches right and levels out. From here the way climbs gradually, twisting through the pines; the narrow path is always curving, and always gently rising or falling.

The last part of this trail joins the Blue Loop and is mostly a wide, easy downhill run back to the parking lot. Watch for the longer trails that merge from your left near the end of this trail.

ORANGE (AND VARIATION)

Length: 9.9 km
Time: 2¹/₂ hours
Level: Expert

The Orange Trail is the main loop trail at Ganaraska. The route leads up into the hills, winds through upland forest, and then descends to the trail centre. Three other trails, the A, B and C loops, add variations to the basic route. These are expert-level trails and will make a good day's outing for all but the most ambitious skiers.

Detailed Tour

The Orange Trail, like all the trails here, starts out with two ways to get past the hill, the advanced or the intermediate route. Once you are on the trail itself, the first kilometre is an almost continuous climb, mostly fairly easy but with a couple of steep sections. At the top of the ridge the way is level, then it drops down in an easy, straight run before entering a reforested area. Here the Blue Trail branches to the right, and soon after this the A Loop also goes off to the right.

The trail climbs deeper into the forest, winding through mature pines. About half a kilometre on, you come to the start of the B Loop. Here you must decide how far you want to ski. If you choose the B Loop you will add about 4.5 km to your outing.

If you decide to continue on the Orange Trail, you will find the terrain continues much as before. This is all very scenic skiing. After you pass the branching for the B Loop, and then the C Loop, the Orange Trail climbs fairly sharply out of the pine woods into an area of young, upland hardwood forest. This forest continues until you come to a major trail intersection where the Orange Trail joins the A and C loops.

From here the way rises slightly through mixed forest until it comes to a very steep downhill. There is a sign warning you to be careful. The hill is straightforward enough, but watch out for the very narrow and sharp right-hand turn. If the weather is cold and the snow fast, this can be a tricky spot.

The trail curls its way back up to an open lookout area. From here you can see over much of the forest to the northwest. The view seems to go on forever, and there is no sign of human habitation.

Past the lookout it is all easy and mostly downhill, with one very long, straight downhill section that makes up for all your earlier climbing. Shortly after the Blue and Yellow trails merge with the Orange Trail, you come to the parking lot.

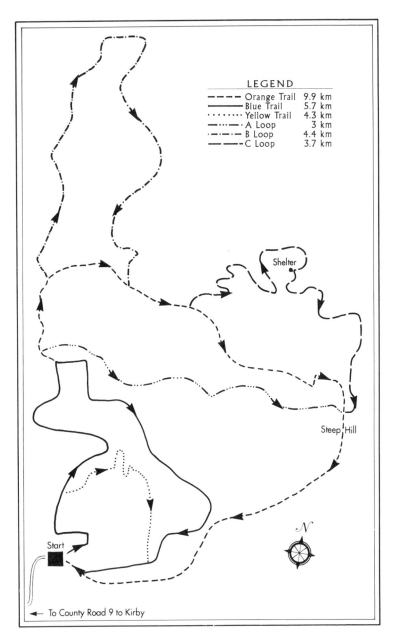

LEGEND
- – – – Orange Trail   9.9 km
- ——— Blue Trail   5.7 km
- ·········· Yellow Trail   4.3 km
- —··— A Loop   3 km
- —·—·— B Loop   4.4 km
- —–—– C Loop   3.7 km

Shelter

Steep Hill

$\mathcal{N}$

Start

To County Road 9 to Kirby

GANARASKA FOREST CENTRE

Cautions

There is one quite steep hill on this trail, with a sharp turn halfway down. If conditions are fast or icy this hill should be skied with caution. There is a warning sign at the top of this hill.

Variations

A Loop: The A Loop reduces the length of the trail to about 3 km. It generally parallels the central part of the Orange Trail through upland hardwood forest. There is one long uphill climb that seems as if it will never end. Don't be disappointed when, at the top, you find yourself on a mainly level plateau. The downhill part does come eventually, but not until you are back on the main Orange Trail.

B Loop: According to the trail map, the B Loop adds about 4.5 km to the route, but it always seems longer than that to me. The first part of the B Loop is the least interesting part of all the trails here. For almost a kilometre it crosses a bald area of scrub bushes and rows of newly planted pine trees sprouting through the snow. This is a reminder of how fragile the forest ecosystem is. Fortunately this sad area is soon left behind and you enter an area of more mature trees, including some areas of large hardwoods. The route continues through the forest until it rejoins the Orange Trail.

The B Loop adds nothing but distance to your outing. If you want to do the extra distance, a better plan might be to ski the Orange Trail and return to the trail centre for lunch or a snack, and then ski the Yellow or Blue trails.

C Loop: This loop adds about 1.5 km to the route and is much prettier than the B Loop. It starts out by climbing sharply and then winds back and forth through a mixture of pine and hardwood forest. About halfway along this trail there is an outhouse and a bit of a shelter, but the shelter offers no real amenities or warmth.

Gravenhurst
KOA Nordic Trails

Gravenhurst KOA Nordic Trails is part of a year-round campground; it offers 17 km of cross-country ski trails, and winter camping by appointment. This is a good place for family outings, with trails to suit all levels of skiers.

Location

Gravenhurst KOA is located off Highway 11, about halfway between Gravenhurst and Bracebridge. Take Highway 400 north to Barrie. Just past Barrie follow Highway 11 north to Orillia, Gravenhurst, and Bracebridge. About 4 km past Gravenhurst watch for the KOA sign on your right. The ski centre is on your left, about a kilometre after you leave the highway.

Paul Cook
RR 3
Gravenhurst, Ontario
P1P 1R3
(705) 687-2333

Topography

The terrain is typical of this part of Muskoka. The ski area is on the Canadian Shield and is mainly flat and wooded, with some hills and granite outcroppings. Spruce and hemlock are the predominant species here, with fewer large mature hardwoods than there are farther south.

Trail Map

The trail map is very good and shows a lot of detail. The distances from point to point are all well marked, so you can plan your route with confidence.

Facilities

The winter facilities consist of eight groomed trails, all wide and double-tracked, with a skating section in the middle. A small store provides ski rentals and some groceries and supplies for campers. A limited choice of sandwiches and snacks is available at the store. There is a large warm-up area in the picturesque old barn at the trail centre and an open warm-up hut on the trails. There are also toilet facilities on the trails.

Cost

The cost of a trail pass is $7 for adults and $3 for children. Ski rentals are available for $18.

Special Features

Call ahead for winter camping, either in mobile homes or in a couple of unheated camping cabins. If you are a devoted camper and enjoy cross-country skiing, this could make a great place for a cold-weather expedition. Bring your mobile home or lots of warm sleeping bags and a camp stove for a dandy winter weekend.

ALL TRAILS

Length: 17 km total

A glance at the trail map for the Gravenhurst KOA will show you that everything is interconnected and there is no single route that will take you out and back to the ski barn. You can pick any one of a number of routes, skiing several trails for each route to give you the right mix of distance and difficulty.

In general, the trails are easy and flat, with a couple of interesting loops. All trails begin at the parking area across the road from the ski barn. To get to any of the trails you will have to cross a short open area that is exposed to all winds. Apart from this, all the trails are in deep forest and well sheltered from the wind. All trails are double-track set with a skating area in the middle.

Detailed Tour

MUSKOKA ROAD: 1.4 KM

This flat trail will be the start of most ski outings here. It winds through deep mixed forest, mostly balsam and hemlock at first, then hardwood. There is a rustic toilet facility at the end of this trail.

MARSH TRAIL: 1.6 KM

The Marsh Trail parallels the Muskoka Road Trail and leads back toward the ski barn. It is all flat and skirts the edge of a large marsh area. There are some very pretty sections on this trail, where spruce and hemlock provide a dark contrast to young hardwood forest. Occasionally you can see over the marsh on your right, where frozen cattails and grass hummocks poke through the snow.

PETERSON ROAD: 1.3 KM

The Peterson Trail, which is also flat and easy going, runs through mixed forest from the Muskoka Road Trail to the warm-up hut. The warm-up hut sits at the edge of the marsh area, and when I was there so was the largest and tamest flock of chickadees I have ever encountered. The air seemed alive with these tiny birds, and when I stood still they even landed on my shoulder. The hut itself is an open, comfortable shelter with a stove and ample firewood.

TAMARACK TRAIL: 2 KM

The Tamarack Trail passes through lowland forest and skirts the edge of the marsh. It is all flat and provides the shortest route from the warm-up hut back to the ski barn.

INSIDE TRACK: 1.6 KM

The Inside Track parallels the Peterson Road, with a few more ups and downs, from the warm-up hut back to the junction of the Muskoka Road Trail and the Marsh Trail. There are usually a lot of deer tracks on this trail.

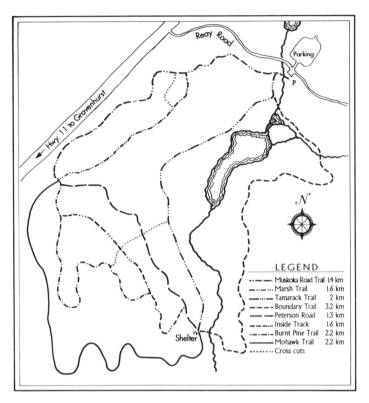

GRAVENHURST KOA NORDIC TRAILS

BURNT PINE: 2.2 KM

The Burnt Pine Trail also goes from the warm-up hut to the Muskoka Road and Marsh trails. It crosses some higher ground and has enough hilly sections to provide a challenge to the novice skier as well as interest for the intermediate skier. It branches off from the Inside Track and winds through forest a bit before climbing a gentle ridge, then eventually drops back down to join the last part of the Inside Track.

MOHAWK TRAIL: 3.2 KM

The Mohawk Trail loops from the warm-up hut to the Muskoka Road and Marsh trails. It climbs and descends a couple of ridges, always in the trees, enough to provide good skiing for intermediate skiers.

BOUNDARY TRAIL: 3.2 KM

The steepness of the hills on this trail will challenge the intermediate skier. Cross an open area to the left of the parking area to reach the Boundary Trail where it enters the forest and climbs steeply up a high bluff. It meanders along the top of the bluff, occasionally providing fine views across the marsh, then drops sharply down the side of the hill to the marsh and the warm-up hut. Experienced skiers will find this the most interesting skiing at Gravenhurst KOA.

Suggested Routes

Novice skiers will find that the loop of the Muskoka Road and Marsh trails provides an easy 3-km outing that can be covered without difficulty in less than an hour. They will find no great challenges but will ski through some very pretty forest areas.

More ambitious skiers can add the Peterson Road and either the Inside Track or the Burnt Pine Trail to this loop. This extension will take just over an hour and will take you to the warm-up hut, where you can break for a rest and enjoy the birds.

Experienced skiers will want to follow the Boundary Trail, the Mohawk Trail and then the Marsh Trail for an 8-km route that will take a couple of hours. This will provide a good workout with enough ups and downs and lots of pleasant scenery.

Hardwood Hills

Hardwood Hills is a World Cup-class facility dedicated solely to providing the finest-cross country skiing possible. A World Cup race was held here in 1991, and the Canadian National Championships were held here in 1993. The focus is on providing the best facilities, trails and snow conditions for each skier who comes to Hardwood Hills, no matter what the individual's level of experience.

Location

Hardwood Hills is located north of Barrie on Doran Road. The distance from Toronto is 100 km, about $1^{1}/_{2}$ hours. Take Highway 400 north past Barrie and turn right at Doran Road, Exit 111. Cross Highway 93 at Dalston and drive 8.4 km, through the tiny village of Edgar, and watch for the sign and ski area entrance on your left.

Hardwood Hills Cross Country Ski Centre
RR 1
Oro Station, Ontario
L0L 2E0
(705) 487-3775
FAX (705) 487-2153

Topography

Hardwood Hills, as the name suggests, is all mature hardwood forest. The hills are generally short and sometimes very steep.

The area is laid out in two sections; the Olympic trail system and the recreational trail system. The Olympic system is meant for the competitive or experienced recreational skier; the recreational system is less demanding, both physically and technically. There are no really long climbs here, and no long, easy descents. Except on the Pine Trail, on the recreational system, there is not much level ground either.

Trail Map

The trail map at Hardwood Hills appears confusing at first, but it is excellent and very complete. All the loops and twists of the trails are shown. Study the trail map for a few moments and the basic layout of a main loop with side loops branching off it becomes apparent.

Many sections and features of the trails are identified by name on the map, such as Little Dipper or Stairway to Heaven, and signs on the trails identify these features. This makes it easy to locate yourself on the map, and is much more interesting than a numbering system. The recreational trails have a good number of You Are Here maps.

All trails are rated on a scale of 1 to 10 for both physical difficulty and technical difficulty.

Facilities

There are over 25 km of trails at Hardwood Hills, groomed for both the classic and skating techniques. On both the recreational and Olympic systems, trails are laid out with a main trail that loops out from the chalet and back again. The recreational section has three additional loops; the Olympic system has four. Numerous shortcuts will eliminate some of the longer sections on both systems.

A snack bar at the ski centre offers quick lunches and hot and cold drinks. There is lots of seating and a table area inside the ski centre, and the covered picnic area outside is very pleasant on warm, sunny days. Lockers are available at the ski centre.

There are over 350 sets of high-quality, well-maintained skis available at the rental shop. A rent-to-buy program allows you to deduct rental fees from the purchase price of new poles, skis and boots. The retail outlet in the chalet offers a complete range of skis, equipment, waxes, and accessories, including clothes and racing ski suits. There is a wide selection of waxes available, and the staff are friendly and knowledgeable.

Behind the chalet is a large, heated hut with about twenty-four waxing jigs and irons available for your use. This is the largest and best waxing facility I have ever been in.

A health club attached to the ski centre has a sauna, hot tub, showers and a separate eating and lounging area for club members.

Cost

The cost of a day pass ranges from $12.50 for an adult full-day pass to $4.50 for a child's half-day pass.

Special Features

There are snowmaking facilities at Hardwood Hills, and that creates a longer season than normal, usually from the end of November until the first part of April. The trail-grooming methods are very high tech, using huge power-tiller groomers that can condition a trail in one pass.

On the recreation trails there are a number of stopping places, each with a picnic table and an outdoor toilet, somewhat primitive but sometimes welcome. Put a lunch or a Thermos of something hot in your backpack, and these picnic spots provide a welcome break.

There is a full program of special events, ranging from a Christmas party with Santa out on the trails to a Valentine's event for sweethearts. The area is open for night skiing until 9:30 PM on Wednesdays. Headlamps are available at the rental shop to make night skiing safer and more enjoyable.

There is a nine-week Jackrabbit program of fun and instruction for children ages five to twelve.

RECREATIONAL TRAIL SYSTEM

Length: 4 km, with additional loops that bring
the total length to 10.5 km
Time: 1–2 hours
Level: Novice to expert
On all parts of the recreational trail system the slower skiers
have the right of way. If you want to pass someone, let them
know that you are there, and then pass without disrupting them.

Detailed Tour

PINE TRAIL: 4 KM

This is the basic novice trail at Hardwood Hills; it is rated with
a physical difficulty of 4 and a technical difficulty of 4. From the
chalet, follow the green signs to the start of the Pine Loop. You
start with a short, level run of two-way traffic. Where the trail
splits, follow the signs for the right fork. The trail is slightly uphill
until you come to a picnic table and toilet at the Posts.

Just after the Posts, there is a shortcut that takes you back to the
Home Run, the final section of trail leading back to the chalet. If
you take this shortcut your entire excursion will be only about 2 km.

Beyond the shortcut the trail winds into an area of small hills
with some short climbs and descents. None of the climbs or
descents are beyond the capability of a beginning skier, although
some are moderately steep.

After the Little Dipper the trail enters an area of reforested
pine woods, then comes to the branch for the Beaver Pond
Loop. The Pine Trail climbs slightly here and after about half a
kilometre meets the branch for Kim's Loop. Here the shortcut
from the Posts rejoins the main Pine Trail. The run from here to
the chalet is easy and downhill all the way.

BEAVER POND LOOP: 2 KM

The Beaver Pond Loop is a 2-km trail that crosses some open
areas and has one good downhill run and a moderately stiff climb.
Both physical and technical difficulty are rated 5.

This loop starts with a straight section, mostly climbing. Another shortcut avoids a long downhill run and climb back up again. The path here is quite open and can be exposed in cold, windy weather. George's Hill is a long, easy run through an open area, with a turn at the start of the downhill. Enjoy the run here, because the next section is called Stairway to Heaven.

The Stairway to Heaven is not as intimidating as its name implies. It is a long climb, of course, but not steep, and there is a picnic table where you can rest at the top. From here the Beaver Loop continues winding through hardwood forest, back to the Pine Trail.

KIM'S LOOP: 3.5 KM

Kim's Loop is a 3.5-km trail that provides the most interesting skiing on the recreational trails. Don't bypass it unless you are really pressed for time or energy on the Pine Trail. Both physical and technical difficulty are 8. A couple of shortcuts can cut some distance off this trail. The forest on Kim's Loop is all young hardwood and very pleasant to ski through.

Kim's Loop, named for Kim Viney, co-owner of Hardwood Hills, starts with the Corridor, a section with lots of small hills and twists that ends at the Straightaway, a shallow grade leading to the Rapids.

The Rapids are a series of very short dips leading down into a tiny valley. There are no difficult turns here. After the Rapids you climb back out of the valley to the Hook, a sharp turn to the left. There is a shortcut that bypasses the next section. After the Hook you come to the Runway, a longer and steeper hill than the Rapids. You may want to slow down in places to keep your speed under control.

Now you pay the price for all the nice downhill going. The Grind is a long climb, not too steep, that will tax the legs and stamina of some skiers. An average skier will do the climb in 5 minutes, without stops. Novices or skiers who are not in shape can count on an 8-to-10-minute climb.

The trail then swings right and again comes to a series of short up-and-down sections leading to the branch for the Lookout Loop.

Passing the Lookout Loop you come to a series of three steep downhill runs named after Donald Duck's nephews, Huey, Dewey and Louie. These are all fast. The first one, Huey, looks quite fearsome from the top, particularly as there is a turn to the left near the bottom. The next downhill is Dewey, just as steep but not so long. If you keep your speed up, you can glide almost to the top of Louie.

From Louie, the trail swings sharply left, then right again to start the last climb. This uphill is not as steep as the Grind, and not nearly as long. At the top, a level section brings you to the end of Kim's Loop, where you rejoin the Pine Trail at the beginning of the Home Run, downhill all the way to the chalet.

LOOKOUT LOOP: 1 KM

The Lookout Loop is a 1-km trail that provides the most difficult skiing on the recreational trail section. It is quite short and a strong average skier can ski it in about 8 minutes. Both physical and technical difficulty are 10 and there are no shortcuts available. The terrain on the Lookout Loop is all open and exposed to any cold wind that may be blowing, but the Lookout at the top of the loop provides a fantastic view.

Branching off of Kim's Loop is a very short, easy climb to the Lookout itself, where a picnic table is usually half buried in the snow. If there is any wind blowing, the trail can drift in a hurry, so you may find the set tracks buried under new snowdrifts.

From the Lookout, the trail continues level for a short distance, then drops quickly down the side of the hill in a steep, fast run with a turn at the bottom. It is not the steepness of the run that gives this trail a difficulty rating of 10, but the possibility that the groomed trail may be lost under fresh snow. It is a nice run and goes for about a quarter kilometre.

From the bottom the route is just a continuous climb back up to where it joins Kim's Loop, almost where it left it.

Cautions

The entire Lookout Loop is quite exposed to wind and drifting snow, and even though it is very short, there is a danger of frostbite during extremely cold and windy weather.

OLYMPIC TRAIL SYSTEM

Length: 7.5 km, with additional loops that bring
the total length to 15 km
Time: 1¹/₂–3 hours
Level: Expert

I was skiing this trail system the day before the Canadian
National Championships were to begin, so many of the com-
petitors were out practising, and testing waxes, and they were
lapping me as I plodded my way around the main loop. They
were all very nice and smiled as they went skating past me, up
the steepest of hills! But don't ever feel intimidated just because
someone faster or stronger than you is out on the trails. Cross-
country skiing has room for skiers of all levels and ages.

Detailed Tour

The basic trail here is the Hardwood Trail, a loop of 7.5 km
that consists of a long series of dips and hills that twist and wind
through mature hardwood bush. There are two shortcuts, called
Racer Out, that provide an easier beginning to the trail.

After about 4 km you come to the Eliminator Loop. This
moderately difficult 2-km loop, with a difficulty rating of 9,
continues over the same type of terrain as the main trail. After a
steep descent with a turn at the bottom, it continues to climb
and descend until it turns and parallels the road, then climbs
back up to rejoin the Hardwood Trail.

After the Eliminator, the way seems easier for a while,
although there is no letup on the climbing. About a kilometre
farther, the Roller Coaster Loop branches off to the right and
rejoins the trail almost exactly where it left it. This 3-km run is
much like the Eliminator in difficulty.

After the Roller Coaster, the route is fairly level for a while,
but eventually it begins climbing, coming at last to the DVP
Loop. This is Dave Viney's Purgatory, named after co-owner
Dave Viney. This very short run has a difficulty level of 10+. It

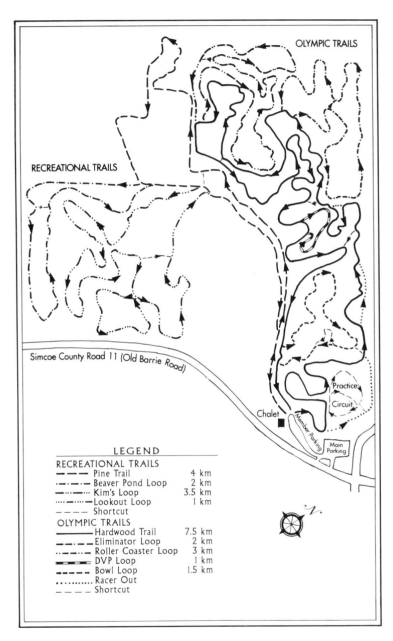

OLYMPIC TRAILS

RECREATIONAL TRAILS

Simcoe County Road 11 (Old Barrie Road)

Chalet

Practice Circuit

Member Parking

Main Parking

LEGEND

RECREATIONAL TRAILS
— — —	Pine Trail	4 km
—·—·—	Beaver Pond Loop	2 km
—··—···	Kim's Loop	3.5 km
····—···—	Lookout Loop	1 km
— — —	Shortcut	

OLYMPIC TRAILS
————	Hardwood Trail	7.5 km
—··—·—	Eliminator Loop	2 km
···—··—·—	Roller Coaster Loop	3 km
▬▬▬	DVP Loop	1 km
—·—·—·	Bowl Loop	1.5 km
··········	Racer Out	
— — —	Shortcut	

HARDWOOD HILLS

begins with a short, steep climb up Heart Attack Hill, then a swift descent into the Black Hole, and ends with a steep climb back up to the Hardwood Trail.

Soon you come to a junction with the recreational trail system. Be sure to keep left here as you go whizzing down the hill. By the time you see the junction it is usually too late to stop and look at the map to figure out which way to go.

After a couple of moderate climbs, the trail straightens out for about half a kilometre, mostly mild downhill, before branching off to the Bowl Loop. This loop is 1.5 km long and has a difficulty rating of 10. It circles around inside the main loop and contains some very steep sections, although nothing as steep and long as the descent into the Black Hole.

After you climb out of the pit to rejoin the Hardwood Trail, you have less than half a kilometre to go to the trail centre, all an easy and welcome glide down.

Cautions

There are no specific cautions noted for this trail system, but be aware that this is a World Cup-class set of trails, and be prepared for some very steep downhill runs and equally steep climbing sections. Still, there is nothing here beyond the capability of an experienced recreational skier.

This trail system is used by racers and aggressive skiers who will often be skiing very quickly. Be prepared to step aside and let these faster skiers past; they have the right of way.

D. McW.

Horseshoe Resort

Horseshoe Resort is a very modern and high-tech facility offering complete amenities to downhill and cross-country skiers of all kinds. Whatever you want you can find here. Although not the least expensive area to ski, it is very good, and you get what you pay for.

Location

Horseshoe Resort is located on the Horseshoe Valley Road, east of Highway 400. The distance from Toronto is about 125 km; driving time is about $1^{3}/_{4}$ hours. Take Highway 400 north to Barrie, then north toward Midland. Turn right at County Road 22 (Horseshoe Valley Road) to Craighurst. At Craighurst go straight ahead about another 3 km, then at the bottom of Horseshoe Valley turn left into the cross-country ski area. If you turn right you will go to the alpine area, where the main hotel is located.

Horseshoe Resort
P.O. Box 10
Horseshoe Valley
RR 1
Barrie, Ontario
L4M 4Y8
(705) 835-2790
Toronto direct (416) 283-2988

Topography

The ski area here is laid out in the valley. On the valley floor the terrain is quite flat and level, but once you begin climbing the sides you quickly find yourself in much more challenging surroundings, with long, hard climbs interspersed with fast, steep downhills. From cedar and hemlock bush in the bottom of the valley, you ski up through stands of reforested pine to open hardwood maple and oak woods. The trails are arranged in three general areas: The north section tends to be the most rugged; the west is flatter and easier, with the exception of the aptly named Heart Attack Hill; and the south trails are all groomed for skating.

Trail Map

The trail map at Horseshoe Resort is very good and has a helpful grid scale so you can judge distances. Routes are clearly colour coded on the map and on the trail signs. Near the trail centre, where all trails follow the same route, the map details can be a bit confusing, but away from the centre all becomes clear. Any important notices of conditions on the trails are posted on the large trail-map board at the centre.

Facilities

There are eleven trails at Horseshoe Resort, covering a total of 31 km. About 22 km of the trails are groomed for the classic technique, and the remaining 9 km are groomed for both classic and skating techniques.

The snack bar upstairs at the cross-country ski chalet provides fast food and a place to sit by a warm fire. There are good washrooms at the chalet, but no toilets on the trails.

Across the road, the Inn at Horseshoe has full bar and restaurant facilities. The Inn offers luxurious accommodations and includes a cross-country trail pass each day. Call 1-800-461-5627 for reservations.

The ski shop at the chalet offers complete equipment rental, with a large selection of recreational packages and, for a little more money, high-performance classical and skating packages. Renting is a good way to try equipment before you buy. As well, the shop has a full range of equipment for sale, and a waxing and repair shop where the staff will wax your skis with the correct wax for the conditions of the day.

If there is a car left in the parking lot after a specified time, usually 4:30 PM, staff will initiate a search of the trails to make sure that no one is lost or hurt. The cost of the search will be charged to the owner of the car.

Private and group lessons are available in classical or skating techniques, some with advanced booking required. Packages that include equipment rental, trail pass, and lessons are available for novices.

At the time of the full moon you can sign up for a moonlight ski. The package includes skiing, a bonfire and hot cider.

Cost

The cost of a trail pass ranges from $11 for a full-day adult pass to $7 for a half-day senior or junior pass. Seasons passes are available.

Special Features

The first thing you notice when skiing at Horseshoe Resort is the quality of the trail grooming. They use a power-tiller groomer, and the trails are groomed every day. This resort specializes in classic trails. All the classic trails are double-track set, so you can ski side by side, and they all are wide enough that you can pass or be passed with no inconvenience. On downhill pitches there is no track setting; on uphills there is often only a single track set, leaving a wide area at one side if you have to herringbone up the hill.

There are two picnic areas on the trails, with bird feeders and picnic tables. On weekends there is a bonfire at each of these rest stops.

NORTH TRAILS

Length: 1.5–12.2 km
Time: ½–3 hours
Level: Novice, intermediate and expert

Detailed Tour

The four trails of the North Trails section are divided into four distinctly marked routes, identified by colour. Shortest is the novice Yellow Trail, 1.5 km long. Next is the intermediate Blue Trail, 3.7 km long. The intermediate Orange Trail is 5.8 km and more difficult than the Blue Trail. The 12.2-km expert Red Trail provides a real challenge to all but the most expert of skiers.

This tour describes the Red Trail, noting where the other trails meet it.

From the chalet, follow the signs for the North Trails. The trails start out through gently rolling open fields and mixed softwood bush. After about half a kilometre the Yellow Trail branches left. The Red, Orange and Blue trails continue for almost a kilometre through a reforested pine plantation, then begin to climb gently. After another half kilometre the Blue Trail branches off to the right.

At this point you begin a flat section with two-way traffic, which brings you to a picnic area with benches and a bonfire area, where bird feeders attract many species of winter birds.

From here the trail begins to climb in earnest. The Orange Trail soon branches left, then the Red Trail enters a narrow valley of mature hardwood trees and begins a long climb. A half a kilometre farther, you come to a rest area and a shortcut to the return part of the trail. There is still more climbing before you reach the top, where you can afford to stop and rest for a while.

The next section is fairly easy going, but the trail map and signs indicate a steep pitch—enjoy the ride, particularly as it flattens out into about a half-kilometre winding glide down into the next valley.

The trail meanders through bush, then meets another shortcut that cuts off the last loop of the trail. Beyond the shortcut you begin another serious climb, to finally arrive at the lookout and rest area. From here on you feel that you are returning home.

Soon you will join the last shortcut that bypassed the look-out area, then ski a generally climbing section to where the first shortcut rejoins the trail. You come to a steep downhill pitch, then the trail flattens out and is finally rejoined by the

Orange Trail. A short downhill section brings you to two-way traffic again and then back to the picnic area, where you will probably be ready for a rest.

A short distance from the picnic area, the Red Trail branches left, following a 1-km loop over a steep ridge. If you are tired you can avoid the worst of the climb by staying on the Orange Trail. If you elect to continue on the Red Trail you will find that this climb is not as long or as steep as the others. At the end of the climb the trail descends gently at first, then very steeply with a sharp turn at the bottom, where it joins the Orange and Blue trails.

Now you are down on the valley floor again and the rest of the way is quite flat. The trail meanders through mixed bush and open areas until it rejoins the Yellow Trail for the final half kilometre to the chalet, running along the golf fairways.

Cautions

The North Trails are groomed for the classic technique and skating is not permitted on these trails. Watch for the direction signs on two sections of these trails, where there is two-way traffic. The 12.2-km expert trail contains some tiring climbs and four very steep, twisting downhill sections. Be very careful on these sections, particularly the first time you ski them.

Variations

The two shortcuts on the outer reaches of the Red Trail allow you to shorten the route somewhat, and on the way back you can take the Orange Trail home, cutting out one climb and downhill section. If you take the last shortcut, the one that cuts out the hill up to the lookout, be sure to turn left when you rejoin the main trail.

WEST TRAILS

Length: 3.8–9.5 km
Time: $^1/_2$–2 hours
Level: Novice, intermediate and expert

Detailed Tour

The West Trails are groomed for the classic technique; skating is permitted only on the Yellow Trail.

The four West Trails tend to be flatter and easier to ski than the North Trails. Shortest is the 3.8-km novice Yellow Trail. Next is the 6-km intermediate Blue Trail, which climbs partway up the side of the valley, but stops short of Heart Attack Hill. Both the 7-km intermediate Orange Trail and the 9.5-km expert Red Trail climb right out of the valley before descending to the valley floor.

This tour describes the Red Trail and notes where the other trails meet it.

From the chalet follow the signs to the left to the West Trails. The trail leads north on a long, straight section through a pine reforestation area. The going seems easy here because you are travelling slightly downhill; you will pay for this pleasure later.

After about half a kilometre, the path swings left, through more natural and rugged evergreen forest. This is a good place to stop and just listen to the quiet.

Soon the Yellow Trail branches left for the return to the chalet. The other three trails continue west along a flat straight section for about a kilometre, with two-way traffic the whole way. At the end of the two-way traffic there is a rest area where you can relax for a while before beginning the climb out of the valley through mature cedar and hemlock forest. About half a kilometre from the rest area the Blue Trail makes a short loop back to the rest area.

A short distance farther the trail brings you to Heart Attack Hill—a steep climb that goes on for about a quarter kilometre. It is dead straight, so you can see the end of the climb before you start. There is nothing that says that you must do it without stopping, so take it easy.

At the top there is a pleasant rest area with benches, facing south, where on sunny days you can take your skis off, lean back, and enjoy the surroundings. If you have brought along snacks and a hot drink, this is an ideal place to open your pack and rest for a bit. There is no great view here, but the whole area gives the impression of a sheltered amphitheatre.

From here follow the trail signs to the left and begin a long, easy descent. There are places where you can pause on the way down. After about half a kilometre the Red Trail Loop branches to the right and begins to climb, looping up out of the valley and then back down again until you finally arrive back near the rest area at the top of Heart Attack Hill. According to the trail map this loop is only about 2.5 km, but with all the ups and downs it feels longer.

At the end of this loop you rejoin the main trail for the downhill you skied earlier. It is such a pleasant run that it is worth doing twice. Unless you are a glutton for punishment, this time take the left-hand fork at the bottom of the hill and the route back to the chalet.

After the turnoff to the Red Trail Loop, the trail eventually meets the outward bound part of the trail at the rest area, where the Blue Trail also rejoins your route.

From here retrace your steps past the alpine lifts along the flat two-way section. About a kilometre on, the Yellow Trail joins up for the final kilometre back to the chalet. This part, which is one-way traffic only again, is where you begin to pay for the easy going at the first part of the route. The way is now very slightly uphill, just enough that your tired leg muscles will let you know it's time to get back to the chalet.

When you come to a sharp left turn, you are almost there. A short descent through the trees leads you to the parking area, and only another 100 metres to the chalet.

Cautions

There is only one hill of any consequence on the West Trails. This is the ominously named Heart Attack Hill, a moderately long, steep climb at the far end of the two longest trails. This is probably the hardest climb at Horseshoe Resort, but it doesn't last long, and the ride down is worth it.

SOUTH TRAILS

Length: 3.8–9.4 km
Time: $^{3}/_{4}$–3 hours
Level: Intermediate and expert

Detailed Tour

The three South Trails sections are all groomed for skating with only a single track set. The shortest is the 3.8-km intermediate Blue Trail. The intermediate Orange Trail is 5.4 km long, and the expert Red Trail is 9.4 km long.

This tour describes the Red Trail and notes where the other trails meet it.

From the chalet, turn right and follow the signs up the hill toward the highway. The traffic here is two-way. At the road, remove your skis and cross. The traffic on your left is coming over a hill, so there is not much time to see cars approaching.

After you cross the highway, almost immediately you cross a road to the parking lot, and then you are on the trails. The trails on the South Trails system follow the golf course for the first part, running near houses. At the top of a short rise take the left fork to the far side of the golf fairway and start up the hill. You might estimate that the length of the climb here is about a drive and a three-iron shot.

At the top of the hill, pause and enjoy the view to the north, up Horseshoe Valley. Here you intersect the return trail, so watch for skiers coming down the hill toward you. Swing to your left and go down a long fairway and into the trees below, then double back, again climbing all the way.

Here the trail turns left and parallels another fairway for a short distance. The Blue Trail branches right and circles a huge water tower before rejoining the return part of the Orange and Red trails. The Red and Orange trails continue beside the fairway and then cross it and climb into hardwood forest, away from the golf course. You are now entering the prettiest part of the South Trails. There are a couple of short, steep climbs through the woods, matched by equally short downhill runs.

Near the bottom of the alpine slope, the Orange Trail branches right and heads for home. The Red Trail now begins some serious climbing up a roadway cut into the side of the hill. It is not too steep, but it is a straight climb for about half a kilometre. At the top of the climb you are right beside the top of the chair lift.

The Farm Loop crosses a roadway and winds through some flat, open fields with very little shelter from the wind. This is the best skating section of the whole trail system. Near the end of the trail you cross the road and ski along an uninteresting route beside it where the snowploughs will often have thrown a salty mess.

On the Farm Loop you have been skiing on the top of the hill, more or less at the level of the top of the ski lifts. Now you must get down to the bottom! The run would not be too bad on downhill skis, although it is too narrow to do much turning. On cross-country skis it can be daunting, especially at the top.

After the first descent you join the Orange Trail, and after another, easier downhill section, you face a sharp climb up to the old water tower and the junction with the Blue Trail. It is all downhill from here.

A short downhill takes you to where the outward-bound trails intersect. Here you reenter the golf course, but this time going the easy way, downhill. The trail is wide and usually very smooth and well groomed, so you may decide to tuck up and act like a racer all the way to where you cross the road to the parking lot.

After you cross the highway, the return to the chalet is an easy run down the fairway. There is two-way traffic here, but if you are going fast enough the skiers climbing up the hill may jump out of your way.

Cautions

There are several road crossings on these trails. The worst is where all three cross the main highway, Horseshoe Valley Road. The other road crossings are all on the expert trail and they cross quieter country roads.

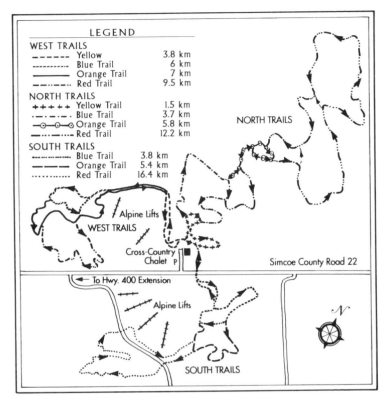

LEGEND

WEST TRAILS
- – – – – – Yellow .... 3.8 km
- .... Blue Trail .... 6 km
- ——— Orange Trail ... 7 km
- — —··—·· Red Trail .... 9.5 km

NORTH TRAILS
- + + + + + Yellow Trail ..... 1.5 km
- ·—·—·—· Blue Trail .... 3.7 km
- —⊙—⊙—⊙ Orange Trail ... 5.8 km
- —···—··· Red Trail .... 12.2 km

SOUTH TRAILS
- ···—···—··· Blue Trail .... 3.8 km
- — — — Orange Trail ... 5.4 km
- .... Red Trail .... 16.4 km

NORTH TRAILS

Alpine Lifts
WEST TRAILS

Cross-Country
Chalet P

Simcoe County Road 22

To Hwy. 400 Extension

Alpine Lifts

N

SOUTH TRAILS

HORSESHOE RESORT

The expert Red Trail has one very fast and narrow downhill run that parallels the edge of the main alpine slope. It should not be undertaken lightly, since once you climb up the expert trail it is the only way back.

The Farm Loop crosses some open, exposed areas; in cold weather, with a strong wind blowing, there is a real danger of frostbite.

Lafontaine en Action

Lafontaine en Action is a year-round family recreation area that has been offering cross-country skiing for many years. There are over 20 km of groomed trails. They extend from the trail centre, just outside the picturesque village of Lafontaine, to the steep bluffs bordering Georgian Bay. Several local public schools arrange ski outings here. This is true cross-country skiing; the trails wind through private lands and county forests, well away from the trail centre. Here you have an objective to ski to, something to do when you get there, and a good ski back home.

Location

Lafontaine en Action is located on Concession 16 in Tiny Township, between Penetanguishene and Lafontaine, about 180 km from Toronto. Driving time from Toronto is about $2^1/_4$ hours. Take Highway 400 north past Barrie, then Highway 93 north to the Midland–Penetanguishene area. Ignore all turns into Midland and go to the third stoplight in Penetanguishene. Turn left onto Robert Street and after about a kilometre turn right onto County Road 26, toward Lafontaine and Awenda. At the stop sign, turn left toward Lafontaine. The ski area is on your right, about 1.5 km along.

Lafontaine en Action
RR 3
Penetanguishene, Ontario
L0K 1P0
(705) 533-2961

Topography

The land north of the trail centre dips down slightly to Concession 17, then climbs steadily to the highest area, the bluffs that overlook Thunder Bay and the islands in Georgian Bay. In

the summer, the area near the trail centre is a campground where trails lead through the woods to the campsites. The rest of the terrain is a mix of natural bush land and reforested areas. The 15-km Senior Trail takes you north to a lookout point above Thunder Bay and to a log cabin warm-up hut in an area of remote forests near the border of Awenda Provincial Park.

Trail Maps

The trail maps here are good and accurate, although they appear confusing at first. The numbers scattered all over the trail map correspond to numbered signs on the trails. This should be a good system, allowing you to pinpoint your location, but I always seem to miss the signs on the trail. However, all of the trails are colour-coded and the markers on the trails are always there when you need them.

Facilities

There are seven trails at Lafontaine, covering 20 km. They offer a real mix of level of difficulty and length, ranging from the .8-km Novice Trail to the 15-km Senior Trail.

The trail centre chalet has a snack bar. There is always a fire roaring in the chalet wood stove, and benches around it where you can relax and warm up after being on the trails. There are washrooms at the chalet and outhouses at a couple of places on the trails. There is a full selection of equipment available for rent at the chalet.

About 3 km of trails are lighted and offer sociable and easy night skiing every Friday and Saturday during January and February.

Cost

The cost of a daily trail pass is $8 for an adult. Children and seniors pay $4.

Special Features

What makes this ski area unique is the scenery. Trails here wind through some of the prettiest land in Southern Ontario.

There is a herd of about forty deer in the woods north of the trail centre. You are most likely to see them early in the morning, or in the evening just before dark.

As its name suggests, Lafontaine is a French community, and at Lafontaine en Action, French is the working language. If you don't speak French, don't worry; the friendly bilingual staff make you feel welcome in both languages.

For something really different, try nearby Chez-Vous Chez-Nous, a bed and breakfast located on a real working farm that dates back to about 1830, operated by Georgette and Jean-Paul Robitaille. There is accommodation for ten people at Chez-Vous Chez-Nous, and all guests are welcomed as part of the family.

Cautions
Some of the trails cross a busy country road. The road is straight and visibility is good, but remember that cars will be travelling at highway speeds.

SKATING (RED)

Length: 11 km
Time: 2 hours
Level: Intermediate

Detailed Tour
This trail is quite challenging for intermediate skiers. You should be prepared for a long expedition.

From the ski centre follow the signs for the Red Trail to your right, first through a level reforested area, then down a gentle slope into a tangle of natural evergreen forest. This continues for about half a kilometre until you come to the first roadway crossing, at Concession 17.

Beyond the crossing, you immediately begin to climb through young, open hardwood forest. The land here is generally rising to the north. This means you will be climbing on the way out and descending on the return trip. It seems as if you will never reach the top of the slope, trekking through hardwood forest to reforested pine, and still farther. This is not all uphill, of course. There are little downhill sections to tantalize you.

Finally you come to the top and have a chance to look out over the gently rolling countryside and find the village of Lafontaine, hidden behind a hill and marked only by the church spire.

The long-awaited downhill run flattens out for a while, then continues down and leads you from the reforested area into a natural hardwood forest. Then it turns to your right and heads north again, mostly uphill.

Eventually you come to Concession 18 and the end of climbing for the day. The view is really spectacular. The entire countryside to the south and west is laid out before you. In the distance you can see the ski hills at Collingwood and Blue Mountain. Ahead of you Concession 19 drops down a steep hill.

The Skating Trail goes down the hill beside a reforested pine area. The slope is not very steep, and runs fairly straight all the way back to Concession 18. This rewarding run winds through pine and hardwood forest, mostly downhill until it again joins the Orange and Green trails as they approach Concession 19.

Beyond the road you cross a very flat area that is swamp in the summer, and then begin a slight climb into the hardwood forest that leads back to the ski centre. Where you come to a fork in the trail, the Skating Trail is the one that goes straight ahead up the hill. Don't worry. There is not much uphill going left.

The trail cuts across a small area of steep gullies marked with warnings to stay on the groomed trails. Suddenly all the trails merge and the ski centre is right ahead of you.

Variations

One of the nicest alternatives on the Skating Trail is to take the Green Trail back from the lookout area at Concession 18. This will add about half a kilometre to your route and will give you an opportunity to ski a skating trail and a classic trail. Go straight down the hill at Concession 18 and turn left at the bottom, as soon as you enter the bush. Don't go too far or you will be on the snowmobile trail. Good signs guide you at the junction.

If you are feeling energetic, instead of joining the Green Trail at the lookout, you could join the Orange Trail and ski another 8 km out to the cabin and back. Afterwards you may hope that there is a hot tub or sauna wherever you are staying.

INTERMEDIATE (GREEN)

Length: 7 km
Time: 1 ½ hours
Level: Intermediate

Detailed Tour

From the ski centre, follow the signs for the Orange and Green trails to your right. The trail is double-track set here and begins by winding through a reforested section of pine. After about a kilometre of fairly level going, a shortcut trail branches left. The Orange and Green trails continue straight and drop down a slight incline into some rough natural evergreen forest. The way continues through this forest for about half a kilometre to the road crossing at Concession 17.

After crossing the road the trail swings right and enters more young hardwood forest. The trail eventually leads up toward Concession 18. This is a long climb with few breaks. Near the top is a bench where you can rest. At the top, the trail turns left and round along the edge of a reforested area, parallel to the roadway. It is exposed to the north, and if there is much wind or blowing snow, it can be a very unpleasant place. On warm, still, sunny days, however, it can be enjoyable to get out of the woods and into the bright sunshine.

After about half a kilometre you come to the top of the hill at Concession 18. Here, where you join the Skating Trail, you can enjoy a spectacular view of the countryside. Far across Georgian Bay is Collingwood and Blue Mountain; in the foreground, the village of Lafontaine is hidden in a fold of the hills.

The trails continue down the hill on unploughed Concession 18. You can stay in the set tracks or ski on the snowmobile trail that runs beside the ski tracks. To stay on the Green Trail, be ready to stop and make a sharp turn left as soon as you enter the bush. The Orange Trail branches off to the right at the edge of the woods and returns here.

After you turn into the bush, the trail becomes a series of downhill runs interspersed with flat areas. There is no climbing here. Some of the slopes are smooth and gentle, and some are fairly steep, but there is nothing an average intermediate skier can't handle with ease. In places the trail is quite narrow with only a single-track set, and sometimes this part of the trail is fairly rough and cut up, particularly if a large school group has been out recently, so caution is advised on the steeper slopes.

It seems no time at all until the Skating Trail joins on your left and you are at the road crossing at Concession 17. Cross the road and pass through a low, flat area that is swamp in the summer. At the first uphill the Orange and Green trails branch off to your right, taking you up through the woods until you join several other trails at the back of the ski centre.

Variations

From the view area at Concession 18, instead of continuing down the road, you can turn left at the house and take the Skating Trail back to Concession 17. This is slightly shorter, and the downhill run is just as pleasant.

If you are getting tired after you cross Concession 17, you can follow the Skating Trail back to the ski centre. It is a more direct and slightly shorter route, but it still has a couple of short, steep, uphill sections.

SENIOR (ORANGE)

Length: 15 km
Time: 3 hours
Level: Expert

This long trail is interesting because it gives you a definite destination at the far end of the trail. However, once you leave the immediate area of the chalet there will be little help available in an emergency. If you injure yourself, or just get very cold and tired, it could be difficult to get back to the chalet.

Detailed Tour

From the ski centre, follow the signs for the Orange and Green trails. The Orange and Green trails are the same from the ski centre out to Concession 18 and back. See the Green Trail tour for details.

At Concession 18, after you have come down the hill from the lookout area, follow the signs to your right for the Orange Trail. When you are coming down the hill, be ready for your turn at the edge of the trees. The trail is set for two-way traffic for a short distance. When you come to a fork, take the left branch. The forest is all young hardwood, and is quite open and bright.

You are still travelling north here, and climbing most of the way, although there are a couple of short downhill slopes. The trail winds through forest with few noteworthy landmarks until you are approaching Concession 19, where you will see a house, with an outhouse at the back, at the top of the hill. The reason for the outhouse becomes apparent when you see the road, which is just a narrow track through the trees—there is no hookup for electricity and no running water.

Once you reach Concession 19, you are at the highest point of this trail. A branch of the trail takes you along a double-set track for slightly less than a kilometre to the lookout point, which is well worth a visit. There is a bench where you can rest and enjoy the view, although it is exposed in north and west winds. From here you look out over Thunder Bay, with Beckwith Island in the background. Beyond Beckwith you can see Christian Island, with Hope Island just poking up at the far horizon.

Leaving the lookout point, you retrace your track back to the Concession road and continue along the main trail for about a kilometre toward the cabin. This cabin is the destination for any expedition on the Senior Trail. There is an outhouse here, and the cabin is a very primitive log structure containing only a wood stove and a couple of benches, but there is a supply of firewood, and if you have brought matches it won't take long to have this place warm and cozy.

When you are ready for the return journey you can take heart from the fact that you have done all the hard work in the first half of the outing. From the cabin home there is very little climbing. Getting home seems to take less than half the time you spent getting there. What a wonderful way to lay out a ski area!

Soon after you leave the cabin you come to a sign that says Danger Hill. It's not clear if that is the name of the hill or if the sign is missing a colon. This turns out to be a fairly steep and narrow downhill section, but if you have come this far, you should have nothing to fear. However, I once saw a pair of rental skis stuck into the snowbank at the bottom of Danger Hill, and ski-boot tracks all the way back to the chalet.

The route continues to wind downhill through the hard-wood forest, back to the Concession 18, where you rejoin the intermediate Green Trail for the final section home. See the tour of the Green Trail for more details.

BONAVENTURE, NOVICE, AND AMATEUR TRAILS

Length: 3 km, .8 km, 1.5 km
Time: $^{3}/_{4}$ hour
Level: Novice

The Bonaventure Trail is a pleasant run that will present no difficulties for any but the most inexperienced novice. It is all double-track set so you can ski side by side and chat as you go. Both the Novice and the Amateur trails are quite level and are good routes for the first-time skier.

Detailed Tour

From the trail centre, follow the signs to your left behind the log house. After a short distance the trail swings right, into a reforested area. This is the summer campground, and there are roadways and signs leading to the various campsites. None of the camp roadways are ploughed during the winter, of course, so the skiing is fine here. This part of the trail is all very flat.

Beyond the campgrounds the trail begins a long, gentle descent into cedar woods and low wetlands. Here you will find the tracks of rabbits and snowshoe hares. Sometimes the deer herd moves into this area as well, particularly if it is a winter with lots of snow, because they find it easier to get around in the dense evergreen bush.

You will also see where porcupines have stripped the trees of their bark. Look for porcupines settled comfortably in the fork of a tree branch during the day. They look like balls of coarse fur about the size of a dinner plate. They do not shoot their quills, so there is no danger.

Soon you enter an area of reforested pine and begin the easy, looping climb back up the slope to the trail centre. Before you know it you are approaching the back of the ski centre, where there is always a place to warm yourself by the stove.

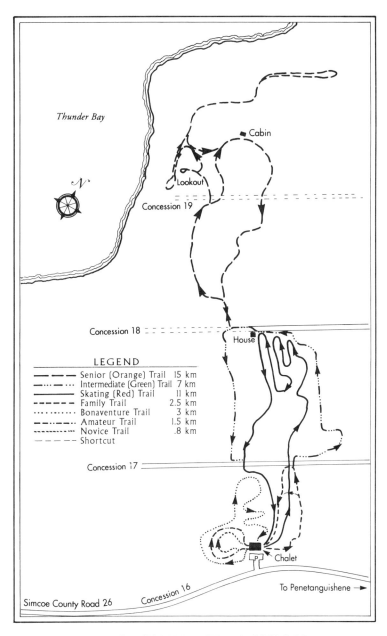

LAFONTAINE EN ACTION

NOVICE TRAIL

The Novice Trail starts out over the same route as the Bonaventure Trail, and soon branches right to complete a short loop within the confines of the summer campground.

AMATEUR TRAIL

The Amateur Trail also starts out with the Bonaventure Trail. It makes a 1.5-km loop, longer than the Novice Trail but still within the confines of the level summer camping area.

FAMILY (BLUE)

Length: 2.5 km
Time: $^1/_2$ hour
Level: Novice

Detailed Tour

From the trail centre, follow the signs for the blue Family Trail. The trail is double-track set and follows the same route as the Orange and Green trails. The path passes through reforested pine. After about a kilometre of fairly level going a shortcut trail branches off to the left, but the Family Trail continues straight ahead and drops down a slight incline into some rough natural evergreen forest and cedar bog. An old boardwalk is used as part of a nature trail in the summer. The path continues through this forest for about half a kilometre to the road crossing at Concession 17. Here you leave the Orange and Green trails.

Instead of crossing the road, turn left and travel beside the road—although it is not visible—on your right. At the turn there is an outhouse, just in case some of the younger members of the family need it.

Soon the Family Trail swings away from the road and crosses an area of swamp and alders, approaching a hill that leads up into a section of open hardwood forest. At the top of the hill the other end of the shortcut rejoins the trail. From here on, the route is fairly straight, with a few dips up and down as the trail passes by some very steep ravines. Join the Green and Orange trails for the last short run to the trail centre.

Long Sault
Conservation Area

The Long Sault Conservation Area is the largest area operated by the Central Lake Ontario Conservation Authority. Winter activities include skiing, hiking and snowshoeing. Many school groups make day trips to the area for skiing and winter outdoor education. There are about 17 km of ski trails. The ski area is divided into two sections: the main area and the secondary east trail. The east trail has a separate entrance and is not used extensively.

Location

Long Sault is located east of Regional Road 57, north of Bowmanville. Take Highway 401 east and exit north onto Waverly Road. Watch that you follow 57 north, and turn right at the conservation area sign on Concession Road 9. The turn into the ski area is on your left, about 3 km from Regional Road 57.

Gord Geissburger
Central Lake Ontario Conservation Authority
100 Whiting Avenue
Oshawa, Ontario
L1H 3T3
(905) 579-0411
Snow Conditions: (905) 263-2041

Topography

The entire ski area is located on top of the Oak Ridge Moraine. This is a significant ridge of high land that was formed by the interaction of two glaciers, and extends from the Niagara Escarpment to the Trent River. The area is generally hilly and is cut by several steep ravines. You will often see deer

and coyote tracks on some of the trails. There is enough variety in elevation to provide interest and challenge to all skiers.

Trail Map

The trail map is adequate but does not show enough detail to help you locate your position on the trails.

Facilities

There are limited facilities at Long Sault. The chalet is used all week by school groups but is open on weekends for light snacks. It is available for groups for a nominal fee, with or without the kitchen facilities. The trails are not groomed or track set, but the number of skiers using them seems to keep them in pretty good shape. There are washrooms at the chalet but none on the trails. There are no ski rentals at Long Sault.

Cost

There is no charge for using the ski facilities at Long Sault.

Special Features

This is a kids' place. I watched a group of grade-school kids heading out one day, and when I asked how many of the mob had skied before, the answer was "none." How lucky those kids were to have the opportunity to get out and enjoy the winter outdoors. And maybe they would come back, on their own or with their families, because they enjoyed it so much!

Also under the same management is a winter activity centre at Enniskillen, only about 5 km from Long Sault. The conservation area at Enniskillen offers about 3 km of cross-country skiing trails as well as a huge toboggan hill and two skating ponds, one for hockey and one for pleasure skating. The ski trail is very pretty in places and makes a fine short outing. It is all quite flat and poses no difficulties. There is a nominal fee at Enniskillen to offset the maintenance of the skating facilities and chalet.

BLACK

Length: 6.5 km (and an extra 1.6 km loop)
Time: 1$\frac{1}{2}$–2 hours
Level: Intermediate

Detailed Tour

From the parking area, follow the trail markers for the Black Trail. You start off in a young poplar woods and soon approach an open area. If you want to take the loop addition, watch for the turnoff to the left across an open area. The main trail continues in forest and soon climbs a steep hill into a reforested area. At the top the 4.3-km Blue Trail branches to the right.

Shortly after, the trail enters dense pine woods and drops sharply down a hill, with a turn partway down. After the loop trail rejoins, the trail swings back and forth, up and down, through a mostly mixed hardwood forest with many scenic sections. The trail is all single-tracked and at times very narrow. Since it is not groomed and track set, there are places where it will divide and go around both sides of a clump of trees. Watch carefully to see where the main trail goes.

Eventually you come to the top of a long, shallow climb and enter a reforested area. This is the high point of the route. From here you go down a long, straight track and finally join the Green Trail just before the parking lot.

BLUE

Length: 4.3 km
Time: 1 hour
Level: Intermediate

Detailed Tour

This trail is not technically difficult, but some novices may find it a bit long. The start of this trail is the same as the longer Black Trail. After the loop trail branches off and you climb into the forest, there is a clear sign showing the Blue Trail going to the right.

The good thing about this trail is that all of the climbing is done right at the start. After you leave the Black Trail, you find yourself at the top of the ridge. Follow it in a series of twisting up-and-down sections through open hardwood forest. None of the climbs or descents are too long or steep, but in several places the trail skirts some steep ravines where you can stop and peer down and perhaps see the tracks of deer or coyotes. Most of the trail is very narrow; in places it is crossed by the tracks of snowshoers or skiers who have decided to break away and go off on their own.

Finally you begin to descend a series of long, easy slopes, and soon the car park appears through the trees.

GREEN

Length: 2.2 km
Time: ¹/₂ hour
Level: Novice

Detailed Tour

The Green Trail is an easy one for the novice skier. It is used by school groups, so it is always well tracked, though there

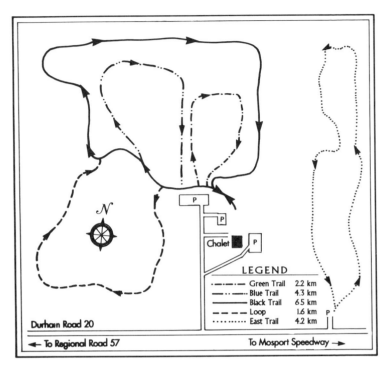

LONG SAULT CONSERVATION AREA

seems to be an unusually large number of small body-sized craters in the snow beside the trail.

From the trail head at the parking lot, the route leads through mainly pine forest. It meanders in a gentle climb and then turns and crosses a reforested area. The last part of the trail comes back down a gentle slope and out into the open, then joins the last of the Black Trail for the short run back to the parking lot.

Mansfield Outdoor Centre

Mansfield Outdoor Centre is a year-round school centre that offers programs on outdoor education and cross-country skiing. For fifteen years it has been providing programs to schools, most based on a $2^1/_2$-day excursion, with teachers and students staying in heated cabins. The programs include both classroom and outdoor activities covering a wide range of subjects, from woodland survival to native tales. During the week the focus is on school programs, but the area is open to the general public for skiing. On weekends all facilities are open to the public.

There are 32 km of trails, all double-track groomed for classic skiing. There is one 4.5-km trail groomed for skating as well. There are lots of shortcuts on the trails, so you can easily choose a route of exactly the length you wish.

Location

Mansfield Outdoor Centre is located on Airport Road, 10 km north of Highway 89, just south of Stayner. It is about 90 km from Toronto; driving time is about $1^1/_4$ hours. To get there simply follow Airport Road north. After you cross Highway 89 you will pass through the town of Mansfield. The centre is on your right a few kilometres farther.

Mansfield Outdoor Centre
P.O. Box 95
Mansfield, Ontario
L0N 1M0
(705) 435-4479

Topography

The ski centre at Mansfield is built at the bottom of a fairly steep escarpment. All trails but the novice Green Trail begin by

climbing up the escarpment to where the terrain is gently rolling, with few steep or severe changes in elevation. The forest cover varies from mixed hardwood to mature reforested pine areas. Except for the White Trail, there are no climbs or descents that will pose any problems to the average intermediate skier.

The trails are all machine groomed and double-track set, but the groomer used here is small enough that it doesn't clear out a broad superhighway through the forest. The trails are just wide enough to allow two to ski side by side comfortably.

Trail Map

The trail map and trail marking at Mansfield are excellent, as you would expect in an area devoted to school groups. There is never any confusion about which trail to take. You Are Here maps at all major junctions leave no doubt about your location.

Facilities

There is a restaurant at the trail centre that opens on weekends, serving the usual hot dogs, hamburgers and sandwiches. During the week, set lunches are available; you will get what the school groups are having that day. That is never a problem, as the menu always includes Joan's "world-famous" homemade soup. I recommend it highly.

There is a large selection of skis for rent. There are washrooms at the ski centre, but none on the trails.

Groups can arrange weekend accommodation for up to about a hundred people. Small groups can stay in the individual cabins, most of which sleep six, and take their meals in the dining hall.

The modern field centre, which sleeps up to forty-four guests in the dormitory wing, is available for mid-size groups who don't want the "winter camping" experience of the cabins. The centre is a separate building and, with the classrooms that are available, is a complete weekend conference facility.

Accommodation at Mansfield is available only on the weekends, of course. During the week it is used by the school groups.

Cost

The cost of a trail pass is $10 for adults and $6 for children. Ski rental is $15 per day.

LOGGER (BLUE)

Length: 9.5 km (7.8 km with shortcut)
Time: 2 hours
Level: Intermediate

Detailed Tour

From the ski centre, start by climbing to the top of the escarpment behind the ski centre. The climb is easy and straightforward. To your left you can see the return part of the trail that you will get to enjoy when you finish your run. This climb is the start of all of the trails here except the Green Trail.

At the top of the hill, take the trail to the right and begin to wind through mixed hardwood and evergreen forest. From here the Blue Trail is mostly level, with only a few moderate slopes up and down. Soon the Blue and Yellow trails branch left and follow a slightly more vigorous course than the Red Trail.

The main part of the Blue Trail crosses the Red and Yellow trails, twisting through mixed forest. The route is mainly level and always scenic. After about 1.4 km you come to a shortcut that will reduce the length of the trail by almost 2 km. The long route is similar to the first part of this trail, with one fairly interesting downhill run. From the shortcut the way continues with a few easy ups and downs. At one point here the trail closely follows the edge of the escarpment, where it drops away in an almost sheer face. There is a fine view out over the valley, but be careful—the drop is steep.

After the main loop, you rejoin the Red and Yellow trails, then the Blue and Yellow trails go off to the right and enter a region of mature reforested pine. About a kilometre farther you cross the Silver Trail, which you can use as a shortcut back to the ski centre.

If you carry on, the trail soon begins to drop down an interesting but not difficult downhill section. The expert White Trail branches off here. Don't take it unless you are competent at steep downhill work. After the main downhill section, the route continues along the bottom of a pleasant little valley and enters an area of large pine trees. From here on, it is all mainly level. If you want to time yourself, it is almost exactly a kilometre back to the ski centre from where you pass close to Airport Road.

THE WHITE TRAIL

The White Trail is a challenging variation of the Blue and Yellow trails. It is a short loop that branches off just before the Blue Trail starts its descent into the final valley. It is off-limits to school groups and is included as a run for the expert skier. It does not add a great deal of distance to the Blue Trail.

After the White Trail branches off from the Blue Trail it continues to climb to the highest point at Mansfield. When you come to a sign that says Caution, Steep Descent, you had better believe it! The hill starts off innocently enough, then turns and gets steeper. Just when you are at about full speed, it turns again and gets still steeper as it begins the main descent. The run to the T-junction, right at the bottom where you rejoin the Blue Trail, is safe enough if you keep your speed under control, but it is not for the faint of heart. Once you have begun the descent you are committed. But it is well worth it!

DEER (YELLOW)

Length: 11.4 km (8 km with shortcut)
Time: 2$^{1}/_{2}$ hours
Level: Intermediate/expert

The Yellow Trail is the longest trail at Mansfield. I classify it as intermediate for technical difficulty, but the length of the trail, particularly if you include the outer part of the loop, requires stamina that may be beyond the intermediate skier. If you try it and find it too long you can cut off the last couple of kilometres and return via the Silver and Red trails.

Detailed Tour

The first and last parts of this trail are the same as the Blue Trail and are described in that tour. This description begins where the Yellow Trail branches off onto a 6.6-km loop.

Just after you leave the Blue Trail, the route climbs gradually through mature reforested pine and enters the Durham County Forest. Soon you come to a very long, wide, level straightaway. This is about a kilometre long, and when you are about halfway through it you may wonder why you ever chose to ski this trail. Just switch to autopilot; the rest of the trail is worth it.

At the end of the straight section there is a shortcut that cuts off the 3.5-km outer loop. Don't take the shortcut. The outer loop contains some of the nicest scenery at Mansfield. It twists and winds through mixed woods with lots of short, easy sections. There is one good, long downhill run you will really enjoy.

There are always lots of deer tracks here. If you are lucky you may see the deer, though I never have. In some places you can see where they have pawed the snow away to get at undergrowth beneath it.

Shortly after you leave the county forest you rejoin the much more travelled Blue Trail. From here on the Yellow Trail follows the same route as the Blue Trail. See the description of the rest of the Yellow Trail, including the White variation, for more details.

LOOKOUT (RED)

Length: 3.7 km
Time: 1 hour
Level: Intermediate

Detailed Tour

You begin this trail with the same long but easy climb as on the Blue and Yellow trails. On the way up, the sight of the downhill run at the last part of this trail may give you energy to get the climb over with.

At the top there is a You Are Here sign to help you familiarize yourself with the area. From here the Red Trail is mostly level, winding through a scenic mixed forest. Early on there is a lookout with a fine view out over the valley. You can see the alpine ski area across the road. The ski centre, almost directly below you, gives you a good idea of how far you have climbed.

At another You Are Here sign, the Blue and Yellow trails branch off. The Red Trail continues through much the same type of forest, young hardwoods mixed with some reforested pine, and about 1.5 km later you come to the top of the hill you climbed at the beginning of the trail and the descent that you saw earlier.

This descent is a fine, wide run down a tiny valley. If there are school groups on the trail, you may find some of the kids walking down, or sitting and sliding down the steeper part. The final, gentle part of this descent takes you directly to the ski centre.

CEDAR (GREEN)

Length: 4.5 km
Time: 1 hour
Level: Novice

Detailed Tour

Instead of starting up the hill with the rest of the trails, follow the signs to the right past the sleeping cabins, to a well-packed area where there are practice trails for teaching beginners to ski. The kids have been skiing everywhere here.

Once past the field you enter the cedar woods. The way is quite straight and level with only the gentlest of grades. It is double-tracked and set for two-way traffic, so if you get tired you can just turn around and start back from wherever you are. This trail is well used. At the end it loops around and retraces the route back past the practice area to the lodge.

This is the easiest of trails and is ideal for introducing beginners to cross-country skiing.

SKATING (SILVER)

Length: 3 km (4.5 km with the extra loop)
Time: $^3/_4$ hour
Level: Intermediate

Detailed Tour

This trail is not used a great deal, but it provides the only place at Mansfield that is groomed for skating.

The first part of the Silver Trail starts out with a gradual climb that gets increasingly steep as it nears the head of a small valley. It will take a strong skier to keep skating all the way to the top. The route parallels the climb at the start of the Red, Blue and Yellow trails, and the return run from the Red and

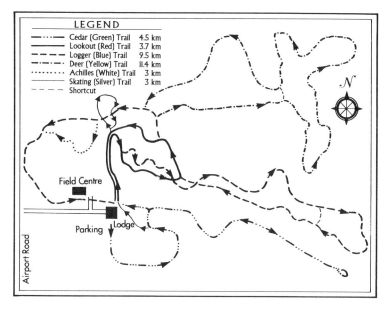

LEGEND
- Cedar (Green) Trail   4.5 km
- Lookout (Red) Trail   3.7 km
- Logger (Blue) Trail   9.5 km
- Deer (Yellow) Trail   11.4 km
- Achilles (White) Trail   3 km
- Skating (Silver) Trail   3 km
- Shortcut

Field Centre

Parking   Lodge

Airport Road

MANSFIELD OUTDOOR CENTRE

Silver trails is right beside it. Keep to the right and watch out for skiers coming down on the other runs.

Once at the top, the route goes through a fairly level area of hardwood forest, crossing the Blue and Yellow trails, and looping around to return to the top of the hill. From here the Silver Trail joins the Red Trail for the final run down to the ski centre.

Midland Mountainview

Mountainview ski area, Midland, is a small, long-established ski area offering both cross-country and alpine skiing. On winter Saturdays and Sundays, and during school break, it is common to see parents dropping kids off for a few hours of skiing, often with both alpine and Nordic equipment. The staff at Mountainview are friendly and create a relaxed, comfortable atmosphere.

The cross-country trails are fairly short but interesting nonetheless. The area is just outside Midland, and in fact there is a large shopping mall within a kilometre of the trail centre. But that certainly doesn't spoil the skiing, and makes it possible to combine a run into town for shopping with a stint of cross-country skiing.

Canadian Olympic skier Angela Schmidt-Foster lives right at Mountainview with her husband, Don, and they both ski the trails here. From time to time she gives lessons to local school cross-country ski teams.

Location

Mountainview ski area is located just outside Midland, about 175 km from Toronto. Driving time is about $1^3/_4$ hours. Follow Highway 400 north past Barrie, then take Highway 93 north to Midland. On Highway 93 you will pass Mountainview Mall on your left. Turn left just past the mall, before the OPP detachment. From here you can see the downhill slopes, about half a kilometre away.

Mountainview Ski Area, Midland
RR 2
Midland, Ontario
L4R 4K4
(705) 526-8149

Topography

The ski area is built on the face of a wooded escarpment facing east toward Midland. To the north the escarpment drops off and forms part of the Midland Golf and Country Club. Some of the ski trails extend into the golf course.

Trail Map

There are no trail maps available here, but the main map board at the trail centre explains the layout clearly. The trails are all colour-coded and the signs on the trails are easy to follow, so the lack of trail maps is not a hardship.

Facilities

Four trails here cover about 20 km of wooded areas, open fields and golf-course fairways. The trails range from the 1.5-km novice run to the 7.5-km intermediate Green Trail.

At the ski centre a snack bar offers fast-food snacks and tables to eat at, but there are no facilities for warming your own food. There are several restaurants in the nearby mall and in downtown Midland. Washrooms are located at the trail centre, but there are none on the trails. You can warm up here at the ancient and rather rustic-looking wood stove.

There is no formal ski patrol, but there are local guides with first-aid training who patrol the trails from time to time.

The trails at Mountainview are double set over most of the runs and are groomed for skating as well. Trails are groomed often and are kept in good shape.

Cost

The cost of a trail pass here is $5 per day. The cost for a day rental of cross-country boots, poles and skis is $12, including a trail pass.

Special Features

Midland's Mountainview ski area may not have the highest downhill runs or the longest cross-country trails, but once you have met Don and Angela and chatted about skiing for a while, you will feel that you are coming back to meet old friends and, coincidentally, do a bit of skiing. One example of the community spirit of the owners is the Wednesday-evening school program, whereby local schools can send their ski teams out to practice and train at no cost.

BLUE (INTERMEDIATE) AND YELLOW (NOVICE)

Length: 4 km (Blue) and 1.5 km (Yellow)
Time: 1 hour
Level: Intermediate and Novice

Detailed Tour

The Blue Trail at Mountainview is a pleasant route that winds across the bottom of the escarpment. The Yellow Trail is a short loop that branches off from the Blue Trail.

From the big trail map across the parking lot from the chalet, go right, across the base of the alpine hill, and follow the signs marked for the Blue, Yellow and Green trails across an open meadow and into young hardwood forest. The Yellow Trail branches left here and circles back through a level forest area before rejoining the Blue Trail back to the chalet area.

Shortly after entering the forest area you come to an area where the Blue and Green trails converge. The Blue Trail continues through the bush in a long loop that returns to the area where the trails meet, then joins the Green Trail and crosses several small gullies at the bottom of the escarpment. There is a short, sharp climb followed by a downhill run with a left turn in the middle that makes it more exciting for novice skiers.

After the downhill, the trail leaves the woods for a short distance, then joins the Red Trail and crosses the bottom of the alpine area to return to the chalet. Watch for skiers coming down the alpine slope as you emerge from the trails.

RED

Length: 5.3 km
Time: 1¹/₄ hour
Level: Expert

Detailed Tour

The Red Trail at Mountainview makes the most of the available terrain and combines interesting scenery with the opportunity for a good workout. This is the trail used for racing and for training the school teams.

After you get your trail pass at the chalet, study the big trail map posted at the bottom of the ski hill. There are no printed trail maps available here, so this is your only chance to become familiar with the route. When you have it memorized, turn left and ski past the chalet to the first Red Trail marker.

The first part of the trail winds through mostly open meadow, within sight of the back of the Mountainview Mall. Soon you turn toward the hills and begin to climb through young hardwood forest. After a short, steep climb you go back down on a nice run. Then begins a long climb to the top of the ski area and the open fields to the west. As you climb you will catch glimpses through the trees of the view to the north over Severn Sound toward the villages of Port McNicoll and Victoria Harbour, and to the south toward Georgian Bay.

At the top the trail skirts the edge of the escarpment on your right; you can see the top of the ski-lift mechanism from here. To your left are open fields, so the wind can get very cold here. Past the ski lift you come to a fork in the trail. The left path carries on across the field and the right one drops down steeply into the forest in a short but exciting run. As soon as you reach the bottom of the slope you will have to climb back up again, but this little diversion provides interest and lots of opportunity for exercise. If you aren't feeling ambitious, take the left fork and ski along the edge of the escarpment.

Where the two parts of the trail join, there is an impressive view across to the ski hills at Collingwood and Blue Mountain, about 55 km away. On a clear day the alpine ski runs there stand out sharply.

Carry on across the open field, where the trail starts with a long glide that has just enough of a down slope to make you look like a real expert in the skating technique. The path bends and gets steeper, then bends again and approaches a steep pitch down to the forested area. Be careful and look for a smooth part of the trail, particularly if the snow is marked by the falls of other skiers.

From here go straight on into the reforested area. There is two-way traffic with the Green Trail, so watch for skiers coming the other way, particularly if you still have speed up from the downhill run.

The Red Trail eventually branches right and climbs gently through the pines before rejoining the Green Trail. The way seems a bit confusing, but the signs soon make it clear. The Red Trail branches right again and crosses the face of the escarpment. The forest is young hardwood and quite open and park-like. If you see some huge, long wood chips here, look around for the pileated woodpeckers that live in this area.

There are tiny valleys cut into the face of the escarpment and the trail crosses three of them. This creates a series of three steep but short climbs, with equally steep descents between them, providing a good challenge to racers and to the teams training here.

Finally you come to the easy slope that crosses the bottom of the alpine section. Watch for the alpine skiers as you emerge from the trails. From here you can glide past the ski lift to the chalet area.

Cautions

Some of the downhill sections are quite steep and should be approached with caution. The open area at the top of this trail can get very cold if there is a wind blowing from the west or north, so be aware of the potential for frostbite.

Variations

When you come down the long hill before entering the straight section of reforested woods, turn sharply right and join the Green Trail for another short climb and more interesting scenery than you will find in the reforested pine woods.

If you are getting tired, take the Blue and Green trails at the finish and avoid the three steep up-and-down sections across the face of the escarpment.

GREEN

Length: 7.5 km
Time: 1$\frac{1}{2}$ hours
Level: Intermediate

Detailed Tour

The Green Trail follows much the same route and terrain as the Blue Trail but extends it by including a lot of the golf course.

From the big trail map, go to your right across the base of the alpine hill and follow the signs marked for the Blue, Yellow and Green trails across an open meadow and into young hardwood forest. The Yellow Trail branches to the right here and circles back through a level forest area.

Shortly after entering the forest area you come to a place where the Blue and Green trails converge. Take the right-hand branch and follow it through the forest. Soon you come out onto the edge of the fifteenth fairway of the Midland Golf Club. The trail from here on is wide and groomed for both skating and classic skiing.

The route is level and then begins to descend as it approaches the clubhouse, where the trail forks. The left fork is a shortcut that cuts off a delightful run down the hill and the climb back up again. If you take the right fork, you will continue on down the hill over the length of the first and second fairways. This is a

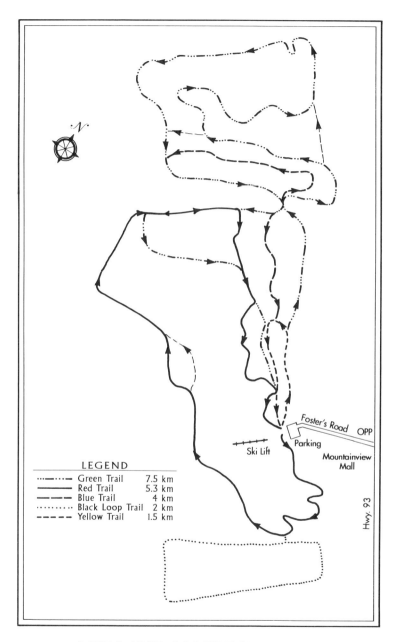

LEGEND
········ Green Trail   7.5 km
———— Red Trail   5.3 km
– – – Blue Trail   4 km
········· Black Loop Trail 2 km
- - - - Yellow Trail   1.5 km

MIDLAND MOUNTAINVIEW

continuous descent, never steep, but never level enough to stop you from gliding smoothly along.

At the end of the run you will find yourself at the lowest point on the route. Fortunately, golfers enjoy steep climbs no more than skiers do, so all of the uphill work is gentle, though fairly long. As you continue around the edges of the golf course you occasionally cut through small wooded areas, all the time climbing steadily. About halfway around the golf course, the shortcut rejoins the route. From here it is only a short distance to where the trail leaves the course and turns right, into the woods.

Soon you rejoin the Blue Trail for a short distance. Following the signs for the Green Trail, ski a long, straight section through reforested pine. (For the last part of this section you are travelling against the traffic on the Red Trail.) As you emerge from the reforested area, the Green Trail swings left and climbs partway up the escarpment before turning again.

This is a pleasant part of the trail, leading through open mixed woods. It winds across the side hill and eventually crosses the Red Trail. The Green and Blue trails join up for a short climb and an easy run down to the base of the escarpment. From here you have only a short way to go through the level forest until you again rejoin the Red Trail and emerge onto the edge of the alpine ski run. Watch for the alpine skiers as you cross the slope to the chalet.

Variations

The shortcut down the tenth fairway cuts out the delightful run down past the clubhouse, and of course the climb back up. Near the end of the Green Trail you can cut some distance by crossing over onto the Blue Trail to follow it home. To add some excitement, branch off to the right and join the Red Trail to ski the three steep sections as the trail approaches the finish area. The roller-coaster ride on this last part of the Red Trail makes a fine short route that will give an intermediate skier a good opportunity to try part of an expert trail.

Minto Glen
Winter Sports Centre

The ski area at Minto Glen is a small, well-wooded site set in a fold in the hills between Harriston and Mount Forest. It is a complete winter sports centre that specializes in catering to families and local groups. There has been ski activity here since the 1940s. Once, before alpine skiing became so sophisticated, there was a rope tow and a downhill run. All winter snow sports except alpine skiing are available here now. This is a great place to come and spend a day just playing in the snow.

Although small, the area offers 10 km of excellent trails that twist tightly through beautiful mixed hardwood, pine and cedar woods. The narrow trails are all groomed and track set; some areas are groomed for skating as well as for classic style.

Location

Minto Glen is about 170 km from Toronto, and the driving time is about 2 hours. Take Highway 400 north and turn west on Highway 9. At Arthur, take Highway 6 north to Mount Forest and go west on Highway 89. Watch for the Minto Glen sign at County Road 2, where the road makes a large bend to the left. The ski area is about 4 km north on County Road 2.

Minto Glen Winter Sports Centre
RR 3
Clifford, Ontario
N0G 1M0
(519) 338-2782

Topography

The chalet at Minto Glen is built right at the top of a north-west-facing ridge. This ridge is steep in places, making for some fast and interesting runs, but this means that you always start

out downhill and finish with a climb back up to the warmth of the chalet.

Trail Map

The trail map is adequate, though it is easy to get turned around and lose your exact position at times. Fortunately the area is small enough and the main trails are well enough marked that there is no real problem.

Facilities

The chalet is also the home of the owners. The warm-up area and snack bar are in the basement of the house, and there is always a warm fire going in the corner. The former downhill slope is now used for almost anything that will get you down the hill. Skis, snowboards, snow racers, sleds, tubes, carpets, toboggans and snowshoes are all available for rent.

Cost

The cost of a trail pass for the day is $4, including the toboggan hill. The cost for using the toboggan hill is $2 per day. Special group rates are available.

Special Features

Church groups, Guides and Scouts regularly arrange ski parties here. The University of Waterloo ski team practises here and the Wellington County Board of Education offers a course on the fundamentals of skiing.

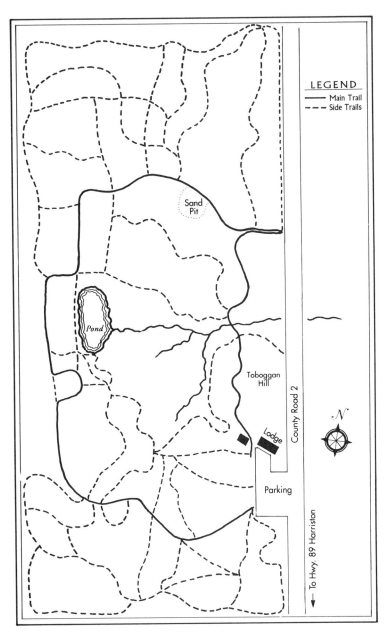

MINTO GLEN WINTER SPORTS CENTRE

ALL

Length: 10 km
Time: Various
Level: Novice to intermediate, with some expert sections

Detailed Tour

The main trail at Minto Glen is laid out in a loop about 2.5 km long. There are many branching loops that intertwine through the woods, so no two excursions will follow the same route. The variety is almost endless.

From the parking lot, the main trail drops down the side of the ridge and begins twisting through mixed woods, mostly pine, with some cedar and hardwood. The bush is dense, so you can never see very far ahead. The going is all up and down, but there are no long, significant climbs or downhill runs.

The end of the main trail comes out at the bottom of the toboggan hill. Several long, steep paths lead up the hill, all winding through forest and eventually coming out into the open area around the chalet. When you reach the top of the hill, if the area isn't very busy, the temptation to take a fast run down can be almost overwhelming. The 30-second run to the bottom is great, but not for the novice or faint of heart. Be careful! Once at the bottom, of course, there is only one way to go: back up the hill again.

This aspect of Minto Glen reminds me of my early days skiing on fields near my childhood home. We would ski down a hill, then turn and climb back up to do it again. That was in the days of bear-claw bindings, wooden skis and no steel edges. Minto Glen is the only ski area that I know of where I would dare try that sort of thing now!

This is not the most sophisticated ski centre around, but if you want a day of skiing that takes your mind back to earlier times, or if you have a whole gang of family and friends of all ages who are looking for a great day outdoors, give Minto Glen a try.

Seneca College, King Campus

The King Campus of Seneca College is a small, partially wooded area on the old Eaton estate, home of the founder of the T. Eaton Company. The ski trails at Seneca are well used. They are really quite easy and are not designed to appeal to the serious skier, but they are still surprisingly pleasant in places, and the location is so convenient and handy to the city. Every winter day, a good number of city kids get a chance to get out of Toronto and try skiing. For some of them, this may be their only chance to see real wild deer tracks and listen to the quiet of the forest.

Location

The King Campus of Seneca College is located on Dufferin Street at the Bloomingdale Sideroad, just north of King City. The distance from Toronto is about 30 km and should take less than half an hour. Take Highway 400 north and turn east onto King City Road. Go through King City and turn north at Dufferin Street. The campus is on your left, just past the Bloomingdale Sideroad.

Seneca College, King Campus
13990 Dufferin Street
King City, Ontario
L0G 1K0

Topography

This area is located on the Oak Ridge Moraine but is nonetheless fairly gentle. The site rises from a couple of small lakes in the centre to a higher, rough area in the northeast corner. Once away from the campus buildings and ski centre, you find yourself in a mixture of open fields and light, open forest.

Trail Map

The trail map is excellent and shows all of the buildings, roads and wooded areas on the site.

Facilities

Facilities here are limited and are geared mainly to the classes of schoolchildren who come here almost every day. There are skis for rent, and there is a large lunchroom. A snack bar is open on the weekends.

There are about 14 km of groomed trails here, with trails for both the classic and skating technique.

Cost

The cost for an adult day pass is $6 during the week and $8 on the weekend. Children pay half price, and family passes are available. Senior citizens ski for free during the week.

Special Features

The imposing former Eaton Hall is an attraction. When I was growing up in this area, "Lady Eaton's home" was a place shrouded in the mystery that surrounds the very wealthy. Now you can ski right up to the house, and even arrange a wedding party here or have a meal in the restaurant. Be sure to call ahead, as the dining room is not always open.

ALL

Length: Various, ranging from 2.1–6.1 km
Time: Up to 1½ hours
Level: Novice to intermediate

Detailed Tour

The trails are laid out in two areas. To the west is the fairly flat Skating Loop, which crosses open areas past Little Lake and circles an open meadow in the forest before returning the ski centre.

The longest trail, the Black Trail, follows the skating trail at first and then branches off into the woods to circle the two lakes

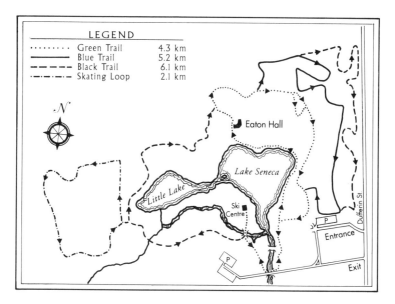

SENECA COLLEGE, KING CAMPUS

before joining up with the Green and Blue trails just behind Eaton Hall. This section is almost all flat.

The shorter Green and Blue trails cross the main campus area before coming down to the edge of Lake Seneca, where they follow the shore to the lawn in front of Eaton Hall. They pass right beside the mansion and then circle through the woods behind it. Soon you come to an old picnic area with a huge fireplace, grill, table and benches, all made from stone.

Here the trails split, and the easier Green Trail heads back to the ski centre. The Blue and Black trails now come to the North Hill, a fairly steep and surprisingly long climb. Parts of this area seem quite remote, and you may see deer and coyote tracks—yes, even this close to the big city.

Beyond the hill the Blue and Black trails split, each taking a separate route back to the edge of the lake and the area near the main campus. This part is a mixture of open fields and forest. At one point you find yourself skiing beside Dufferin Street, where it may seem less like real cross-country skiing.

Springwater Provincial Park

Springwater Provincial Park is a small park that offers family-oriented activities year-round. A unique attraction is the display of native animals and birds. Skiing at Springwater is easy and not really very challenging, but it is always uncrowded and comfortable. Not only can you ski, you can hike the roads and pathways or walk around the animal display area, perhaps pulling small children on sleighs. The play area and swings can be used even in the winter.

Location

Springwater Provincial Park is located on Highway 26 about 100 km from Toronto, 10 km northwest of Barrie. Driving time from Toronto is about an hour. Take Highway 400 north to Barrie, then follow Highways 26 and 27 north about 8 km. Watch for the sign for Springwater Provincial Park, where Highway 26 branches left toward Collingwood. The park is on your left just a kilometre from Highway 27.

Go past the fee station at the park entrance and turn right, following the one-way road until you come to the two parking areas.

Park Superintendent
Springwater Provincial Park
Ministry of Natural Resources
Huronia District Office
Midhurst, Ontario
L0L 1X0
(705) 728-2900 or (705) 728-7393

Topography

Springwater is fairly flat; the ground rises gently from the park entrance to the railway embankment at the southeast border of the park. There is little hardwood forest here. The vegetation varies from tangled natural cedar and balsam woods to stands of seventy-year-old reforested red and white pine.

Trail Map

The trail map at Springwater is only fair. There is a good scale on it, and all of the twists and turns of the trail are shown, but sometimes it is difficult to orient yourself on the map, particularly where the three trails come together. Trail maps are in a little box beside the path at the parking lot.

Facilities

Three ski trails cover about 11 km: the 2.4-km Wildlife Trail, the 2.4-km Woodland Trail and the 6-km Nursery Trail.

All the trails at Springwater are considered novice-level trails. This is a family area, where young and inexperienced skiers can be introduced to the sport, and all can enjoy the displays and other activities.

The trails are not patrolled, and it is recommended that you do not venture onto the trails after dark. Pets are not permitted on the trails, and you are asked not to walk on the track-set trails. Visitors are, however, encouraged to walk and hike on the park roads and paths. Throughout the park area, signs identify the various species of trees, and in the reforested areas they indicate the year they were planted.

The washroom and warm-up huts here are the best of any reported in this book. At the trail centre there is a large, covered picnic shelter that is pleasant on warm spring days. Attached to this area are two solid log warm-up huts, each with a wood stove and a good supply of wood. There is no running water in the huts. A hut can be reserved by calling ahead the day before you come, but I have never had any trouble getting the use of a hut. There is a public telephone near the picnic area.

There are no equipment rentals or snack-bar facilities available. Be sure to bring your own supplies.

Cost

The charges here are for car parking only. The cost is $6 per car per day, or $24 for a season pass to any provincial park from November 1 to March 31. Any number of people may ski on one parking permit.

Special Features

The main feature of Springwater Park is the animal display area. In a pleasant collection of trails that wind through the woods near the trail centre, there are many native animals on display. The trails are fine for either walking or skiing. The animals on display vary from time to time; I have observed a red-tailed hawk, horned owl, timber wolf, white-tailed deer, bobwhite and wild turkey.

WOODLAND

Length: 4 km
Time: ³/₄ hour
Level: Novice

Detailed Tour

From the picnic area, follow the broad pathway past the park office, leaving the washrooms and the animal display areas to your right, until you reach the signs for the beginning of the Woodland Trail. You start up a gentle slope, through reforested red pine woods. After a short distance you will come to the road. Follow the trail to the right, then cross the road and go up a short, moderately steep climb through an area of mainly brush and new forest. At the top of this grade the trail winds along, very gently, until it comes out beside the railway embankment. Good signs mark the route at all times.

After about 200 metres the trail takes you back into the forest, looping through the trees, until you come to a long, slow, downhill section. The trail is often cut up and rutted, so you may have to be careful. As you descend, you pass from the red pine reforested area to a natural tangle of cedar, balsam and hemlock bush. This is the sort of area preferred by deer.

At the bottom of the hill, turn right and join the Wildlife Trail for a short stretch along a flat, straight, double-track section. The forest here is mostly a thick tangle of balsam fir and hemlock. After about 100 metres, watch for the sign indicating your right turn back to the trail centre.

The area around the centre always seems to be crisscrossed with trails and paths not shown on the trail map, so it can be confusing here. Don't worry—all paths eventually lead to the trail centre.

Cautions

Shortly after leaving the trail centre the route crosses the main road through the park. Beware of cars, especially if there are young children in your group. During windy weather some of the open areas beside the railroad track can be exposed and cold.

WILDLIFE

Length: 2.4 km
Time: ½ hour
Level: Novice

Detailed Tour

From the picnic area, follow the signs to the left for the Wildlife Trail. Cross the narrow bridge past the swan pond, where the swans swim in a patch of water that stays open all winter. Turn left again across the open field to the road, and cross the road to enter the woods. Signs will take you to a sharp left turn, then, after a short, straight section, to a right turn into deep woods, where the trail becomes narrow and dark.

From here the trail follows a large loop through the evergreens, crossing several small streams. Take your time on this part of the trail; you will always see deer tracks here, as well as rabbit and fox footprints. The young trees and shrubs provide excellent cover for many animals in the winter.

After completing the loop, the trail joins the end of the Woodland Trail for a short distance, then branches left for the final run back to the trail centre.

NURSERY

Length: 6 km
Time: 1¼ hour
Level: Novice

Detailed Tour

This trail is the longest and most varied trail at Springwater. From the trail centre, follow the signs to the left for the Nursery and Wildlife trails. Cross the narrow bridge at the swan pond, then turn left across the open field to the park road. Cross the park road and leave the Woodland Trail, following the signs for the Nursery.

The trail winds through mixed cedar, spruce and pine woods for about half a kilometre before opening out as it enters a nursery area of small seedlings. This area can be very cold, as the trees provide no shelter.

Beyond the open areas you reenter a mature stand of spruce trees and then come to a deep ravine, where the trail drops sharply and enters a lowland mixed forest area, briefly joining the Wildlife Trail.

If you continue on the Nursery Trail, you will ski through a rugged section of trail that winds around old stumps and fallen trees before eventually climbing to higher ground in a stand of tall pine trees. Here you cross the Woodland Trail before descending to the road through the park. Cross the road and follow the side of the road past the deer pens to the parking lot and the trail centre.

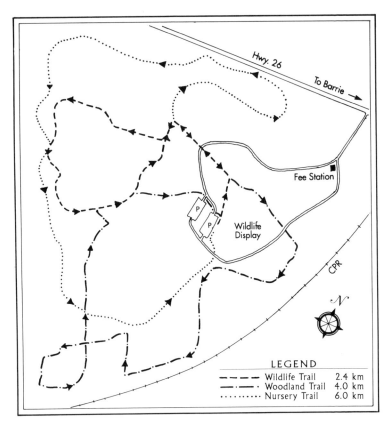

SPRINGWATER PROVINCIAL PARK

Cautions

The first part of this trail crosses some open areas that are exposed in extremely cold, windy weather.

Variations

You can start out on the Wildlife Trail and switch to the Nursery Trail about halfway along the trail, eliminating the rather boring first part of the trail through the open area down into the ravine. This is a better route for beginning skiers.

Wasaga Beach Provincial Park

The Blueberry Plains ski area of Wasaga Beach Provincial Park is fairly small and is utterly removed from the honky-tonk image of summertime Wasaga Beach. In fact, this may be one of the best-kept secrets of the Southern Ontario ski community. There are always fresh deer tracks in the snow within a few metres of the trail centre. You will find deer, birds, porcupines, rabbits and snow fleas, and the absolute silence of the deep woods.

Location

The Blueberry Plains ski trails are located about 18 km west of Elmvale. Driving time from Toronto is about $1^3/4$ hours. Take Highway 400 north to Barrie, then Highway 27 north to Elmvale. In the centre of Elmvale turn left at the lights onto Highway 92. After 18 km, go straight ahead, past the traffic lights and the OPP station, then turn left onto Blueberry Trail. After about 200 metres, turn left again, into the parking lot.

Park Superintendent
Wasaga Beach Provincial Park
P.O. Box 183
Wasaga Beach, Ontario
L0L 2P0
(705) 429-2516

Topography

This entire ski area is composed of ancient ridges and sand dunes laid down about 2,500 years ago, when lake levels were much higher than today. The constant undulation of the trails as they cross the dunes makes this one of the most visually interesting areas to ski. The forest varies, from low, wet hemlock, balsam and cedar groves, almost swamp, to high, dry hardwood

bush at the top of the dunes. Some of the slopes are much too steep and delicate to cross on skis or on foot, winter or summer. The sand dunes and rare plant life make this area unique in Ontario.

Trail Map

The trail map at Wasaga Provincial Park is clear, and, though no scale is shown, the distances from point to point on the trails are marked. The area is so compact and the general trail map is so good that you can easily figure out just where you are at each trail junction.

There is a helpful trail-map board at the start of the trails. Trail conditions are posted on the warm-up hut at the trail centre.

Facilities

There are six trails at the Blueberry Plains ski area, covering about 23 km. These range from the 3-km Skating Trail to the 8.8-km High Dunes Trail, and they all wind through dense woods. All the trails are groomed, and all but one, the Skating Trail, are track set.

Apart from the ski trails, facilities here are minimal. Some ski rentals are available. There is a snack bar and a warm-up hut at the trail centre, where a good fire is always going. The hut closes at 5 PM every day, even in spring, when the days are longer. There is a good warm-up hut with outdoor toilet facilities on the High Dunes Trail, and an open shelter with a stove and toilets at a central point where several trails meet. There are no toilets at the trail centre.

Cost

The cost of skiing here is $8 per day for parking. A season pass for parking admission to any provincial park is accepted as well. These can be purchased at the concession booth at the trail centre.

BLUEBERRY PLAINS

Length: 4 km
Time: 1¼ hours
Level: Novice

Detailed Tour

From the trail centre, follow the signs for the Blueberry Plains Trail. This is an easy, flat trail that loops through hemlock forest where you may see deer browsing. It is double-tracked, which is good for novices, and makes for a very sociable ski outing.

After about .8 km of easy skiing from the trail centre, you will pass a toilet area and warm-up shelter. You will come back here on the return part of the trail.

A further 1.2 km along the trail you come to a short, moderately steep downhill. At the bottom, a trail branches right, to the Red Pine Trail. Follow the Blueberry Plains Trail straight ahead and you will soon come to a rest area equipped with benches, a picnic table, an emergency toboggan, and garbage facilities. The Porcupine Trail crosses here, so if you are an adventurous novice you can take that narrower, more interesting route home.

Continuing past the rest area, ski another .9 km to the warm-up hut, then follow an easy downhill route through thick hemlock forest for a kilometre to the trail centre. Watch carefully; if you are going to see any deer, it will be on this section.

Variations

Shortly after leaving the warm-up shelter on the return journey, you cross the Skating Trail. If you turn right to follow it, you will add about half a kilometre to the outing.

HIGH DUNES

Length: 8.8 km
Time: $2^{1}/_{4}$ hours
Level: Expert

Detailed Tour

Perhaps the prettiest trail in the park, this is a real favourite. The trails here are all one-way. From the trail centre, turn right onto the Skating Trail, a wide trail groomed to permit the skating technique. This part of the forest is dense evergreen bush, mostly cedar and hemlock. You will see lots of deer tracks, surprisingly close to the trail centre.

About a kilometre from the beginning of the Skating Trail, the High Dunes Trail turns off to the right. From here on, the High Dunes Trail is narrow, with only a single-track set. The trail twists and turns through pine forest, constantly climbing and descending the ancient sand dunes. These dunes have a fairly gentle slope on the front face, toward the water, and a much sharper grade on the other side. Since you are climbing away from the water, you find easy uphill slopes interspersed with much steeper downhill parts. The individual dunes are no more than 10 to 12 metres high, so the effect is one of continuous rolling and is never boring.

After a fairly long climb through hardwood forest you will come to the signs of an old rope tow. It is a relic from years ago, when there was downhill skiing here. All that is left are a couple of old car wheels fastened to the trees, and a long overgrown rampway up the side of the hill. At the top of the rope-tow path there is a steep, short climb that takes you to a place where the trail branches. You can take the left fork and bypass the highest point, or continue up another short, steep climb to the lookout point. The view here is good, but there are too many trees to afford a really good vantage point.

From the lookout there is a wide, steep downhill run that the group I ski with calls Faceplant Hill. That is a name we thought up one day when the show was deep and fresh. You can imagine why! This hill is never groomed. It is very short and the snow is usually marked with the craters left by skiers who couldn't handle the slight compression at the bottom. From the top of Faceplant Hill another trail branches off to your right, taking you down an easier but very narrow slope.

After the hill, you continue on an easy descent through the trees, joining the bypass that goes around the lookout and then to a major trail junction with a shortcut that leads to the Red Pine Trail. There is a safety toboggan here. When coming down the hill that approaches this junction, be prepared to stop. Skiers seem to pause to decide where to go next, and they usually block the trail while doing so. Step to one side if you break, as it is difficult to stop on this narrow section of trail. At this point you will have skied about half of the High Dunes Trail, but it is mostly downhill from here.

Following the High Dunes Trail, you again wind your way through mixed pine and hardwood forest, over and around the old dunes.

After a couple of kilometres the trail comes to the longest and steepest downhill part. The descent is no more than 15 metres, but steep for cross-country skis. At the bottom there is a warm-up hut and toilets—a good place to stop. There is dry firewood inside the hut, and even if there is not a fire going when you get there, it won't take long to light one and get the place warmed up. The nails on the beams in the hut make a fine place to dry sweatshirts that have become a bit soggy from the exertions of the trail. If you have brought some drinks or snacks, now is the time to break them out. You can afford to spend some time here, as it will take only about half an hour to get back to the trail centre.

Beyond the hut you leave the hardwood forest behind and follow the trail through pine trees again. The terrain is mostly level, skirting around the end of the major dune area. Near the end of the trail you will join up with the Skating Trail once more for the final kilometre to the trail centre.

Cautions

This is a fairly demanding trail, both physically and technically. You should be able to easily ski the Red Pine Trail before attempting the High Dunes Trail.

MONUMENT HILL

Length: 3.4 km
Time: 1 hour
Level: Expert

Detailed Tour

This trail is an optional loop off the High Dunes Trail. It passes by the base of Monument Hill, a prominent parabolic sand dune with slopes too steep and fragile to traverse with skis or on foot.

About 1.5 km from the start of the High Dunes Trail, you come to a cross trail that is the start of the Monument Hill Trail. Turn right here to begin your tour of Monument Hill. This trail, like the High Dunes Trail, winds through pine and mixed hardwood forest, climbing and descending small dunes, gradually ascending all the time.

About 2 km from the High Dunes Trail there is a sharp left turn. This is a good place for youngsters to climb partway up the hill and send themselves careening recklessly down again while the adults rest and watch. After a couple of runs down the hill, they should be ready to continue.

After a rather flat section, the trail turns sharply right and begins to climb in earnest through a narrow valley with hills rising sharply on both sides.

On those warm spring days when the sun is strong and the snow is soft, you may notice that the snow is covered with tiny black specks that look like soot or pepper. Stop and take a closer look. Sometimes the trail and ski tracks are black with them. These are perfectly harmless, tiny insects called springtails, commonly known as snow fleas. If you look closely you will find that they actually do jump like fleas. As part of their breeding cycle they work their way to the surface of the spring snow, then go back down into the leaf mould of the forest floor for the rest of the year.

Near the end of the climb, the valley opens out and you are faced with a short, steep ascent to the top of the dune. Once at the top, you follow a razorback ridge with the ground on your right falling away in an almost sheer cliff, too steep for even trees to grow to any significant size. To the left the hill drops away on an easy slope to the base of the dune. The razorback eventually turns back upon itself sharply, enclosing a tiny valley with spectacularly steep sides.

From here, one last short climb brings you to the top, and to a very steep descent down a narrow trail. Obey the signs here. Remove your skis and walk down the first part. It is just too narrow and dangerous to ski the first part on cross-country skis.

From here on you get to enjoy the rewards of all your climbing; it is all downhill until you rejoin the High Dunes Trail. Turn right when you come to the High Dunes, and carry on to the most challenging parts of that excellent trail.

Cautions

This is a physically demanding trail, though it is not technically difficult for an experienced skier. There is one hill where you must remove your skis and walk down.

Variations

If you turn left at the junction of the High Dunes Trail, a .4-km trail takes you to the beginning of the Porcupine Trail for a shortcut home. This is downhill and you are going the wrong way on the trail, so be prepared to stop if you meet skiers coming up the hill on the High Dunes Trail.

PORCUPINE

Length: 1.7 km
Time: ¹/₂ hour
Level: Intermediate

Detailed Tour

This is a short, scenic trail that makes a good introduction for the beginner. It also makes a good shortcut home for more experienced skiers who have done the first part of the High Dunes Trail or the Monument Trail.

This one-way trail leads down the centre of the Blueberry Plains Trail. I will deal with the trail in two sections. First, something for novices wishing to move up to something a little more challenging.

Once you have skied about half of the Blueberry Plains Trail you will come to a comfortable rest area with a first-aid toboggan. After a rest on the benches and perhaps a snack, turn left and take the narrow trail up a short hill through the pine trees. You will notice immediately that the trail is much narrower.

The Porcupine Trail winds through the pine trees with short, easy climbs up and glides down the slopes of the sand dunes. Look for trees with bark freshly stripped from the trunk and limbs, a sure sign of a porcupine. Porcupines are often difficult to spot, but they can be found sleeping the day away, heads tucked under their tails, in the fork of a tree limb. They do not shoot their quills, and in fact, when tamed, they can be handled and even petted, but carefully! This part of the trail runs for almost a kilometre and eventually rejoins the Blueberry Plains Trail.

More experienced skiers who have tried the Red Pine Trail can join the Porcupine Trail and ski .7 km before coming to the rest area where this trail crosses the Blueberry Plains Trail. Skiers who have skied the first half of the High Dunes Trail but are not looking forward to the steep hills in the second half can take a

100-metre section of the Porcupine Trail and join in where the Red Pine Trail skiers did.

No matter where you start the Porcupine Trail, you will eventually join the Blueberry Plains Trail near the warm-up shelter. From that point you are about a kilometre—all down a very gentle slope—from the trail centre.

RED PINE

Length: 5.6 km
Time: 1 hour
Level: Intermediate

Detailed Tour

From the trail centre, take the Red Pine and Blueberry Plains trails. The first part follows the novice Blueberry Plains Trail. The going here is wide and easy, with two tracks set so you can ski side by side. The forest is mostly dense cedar and hemlock. Shortly after the start you will pass a rest area with washrooms and an open warm-up shelter with a stove. Don't stop now. You will come back here near the end of the trail.

After about a kilometre, at the bottom of a short downhill, watch for the Red Pine Trail to branch off to the right. There is a rest area and first-aid toboggan at the crossing of the Blueberry Plains and Porcupine trails.

From here on, the Red Pine Trail is narrow, with only one track. The forest changes from cedar to pine as you climb farther into the dunes area. The route climbs easily up the front side of the dunes, pauses at the top, then drops sharply a few feet to another flat section leading to another dune.

If the area is not crowded, be sure to stop and listen to the quiet. It is sometimes hard to believe that you are only a few minutes skiing away from the world's largest and busiest fresh-water beach. Keep a good lookout behind you for faster skiers; it is only good manners to step aside and let them through.

About a kilometre before the end of the trail you will rejoin the Blueberry Plains Trail, where the track is again set so you can ski side by side. After about half a kilometre you will come to the warm-up shelter, a three-sided hut with a roof and a stove. It is out of the wind and surprisingly warm in front of the stove. Look for the firewood behind the hut.

From the warm-up shelter, you go down a gentle slope, leaving the pine woods behind and reentering the cedar and hemlock forest, where you should keep your eyes open for deer. After a short distance you will come around the last corner and arrive at the trail centre.

Variations

There are lots of variations available here. For instance, you can ski the Red Pine Trail out and return by the Porcupine Trail. This cuts some distance off the excursion. You can ski out on the Red Pine Trail and cut over to the High Dunes Trail, cutting out some of the toughest climbing of that trail but touring some very interesting sections. This adds to the length of the basic Red Pine Trail.

SKATING

Length: 3 km
Time: $1/2$ hour
Level: Novice

Detailed Tour

From the trail centre, take the right-hand branch onto a smooth trail that is groomed for skating and wide enough to ski two or even three abreast. This trail is level and never climbs out of the lowland evergreen forest.

The Skating Trail cuts away from the High Dunes Trail after just less than a kilometre and crosses the Blueberry Trail, but it never reaches the warm-up shelter, where most of the

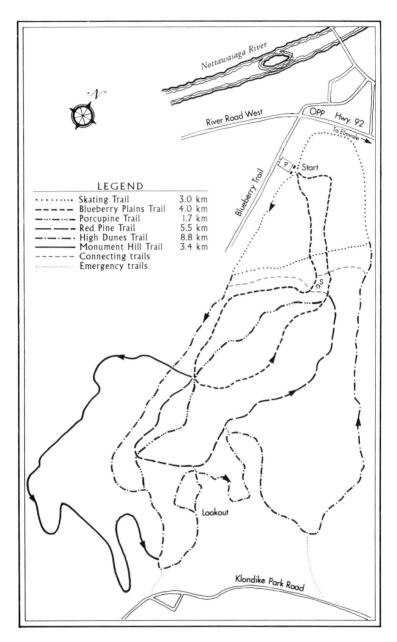

WASAGA BEACH PROVINCIAL PARK

other trails converge. It continues across the ski area and loops back to the trail centre. Apart from the possibility of seeing deer in the dense woods, there is little of interest on this trail, though it does make an excellent route for those who are just learning to ski.

Variations

If you want a short run, you can go out on the Skating Trail and return on the Blueberry Plains Trail. This variation cuts the distance down to about 2.5 km.

Wye Marsh Wildlife Centre

The Wye Marsh Wildlife Centre in Midland is a 1,000-hectare wildlife management area inhabited by deer, coyote, fox, beaver and many other animals. Of special interest are the trumpeter swans, which have been reintroduced to the area. Interpretive signs along the trails will help you appreciate the land forms and the wildlife. The centre offers a year-round natural history program, with naturalists available to provide guided tours of the area. In the winter there are over 20 km of groomed and track-set trails through conifer forests and along the shores of this wetland conservation area. The Visitor Centre includes displays of wildlife found in the area. This is really a place for family skiing, though some local competitive events are held here.

Location
The Wye Marsh Wildlife Centre is 150 km north of Toronto on Highway 12 just east of Midland. Driving time from Toronto is $1^3/_4$ hours. Take Highway 400 north past Barrie, then Highway 93 north to Midland. At the first light take Highway 12 east toward Orillia. Watch for it on your right after the second stoplight.

Wye Marsh Wildlife Centre
P.O. Box 100
Midland, Ontario
L4R 4K6
(705) 526-7809

Topography
The Wye Marsh Wildlife Centre ski area consists of two distinct topographical areas. Part of the trails run along the edge of a marsh open to the sweep of the wind, creating trails with a wide view and flat skiing, and in places winding through

hummocks of frozen cattails. The greater part of the trails run through cedar bush, climbing into pine and hardwood forest. There is little variation in altitude over most of the Wye Marsh, though some of the trails have some slopes steep enough to provide interest to more experienced skiers.

Trail Map

The trail map available at the Wye Marsh Visitor Centre is fairly clear, but it is not drawn to scale. This makes it sometimes difficult to compare trails. The You Are Here maps on the trail are good, but limited; the longer trails just disappear off the end of the maps, which can be a bit confusing at times. There is a large trail-map board at the start of the trail system.

Facilities

There are three main trails and several branch routes and shortcuts covering about 20 km at the centre. These range from a short 1.6-km run through pine woods to an 11.1-km loop that takes you through pines, hardwood bush, across open meadows and through the marsh wetland area. Trails are all groomed and track set. There are several lookouts where you can stop and enjoy a view of the Wye Valley.

Drinks and light snacks can be had in the snack bar, and a wood stove and barbecue pit are available. Rest rooms and a large warm-up hut are located at the Visitor Centre.

Full ski rental is available at a reasonable cost. Snowshoes are available at no extra charge. The ski rental and snowshoe availability make this a good place to come if you have weekend visitors who want to get out into the fresh air for part of an afternoon, even if not all of the party are skiers.

Cost

Admission to the centre is $4.50 for adults and $3 for children. Ski rental is $6.50. Season passes are available at $50 for a single or $70 for a family. Admission includes the Visitor Centre exhibits and all cross-country and snowshoe trails.

Special Features

About thirty free-flying trumpeter swans live in the wild at the centre. Thanks to a successful captive-breeding program, their numbers are increasing steadily. Because this is a wildlife management area, there are many birdfeeders throughout the area. Put a few grains of seed in your hand, then stand very still, and perhaps a wild bird will perch on your fingers and eat from your hand.

Guided moonlight ski tours are conducted once a week during January and February. The Beaver trail is lit by torchlight every Saturday at 8 PM, and you can explore the Wye Marsh at night. You may see rabbits, owls, or even a coyote on this nocturnal prowl. Reservations are required.

There is a movie theatre in the Visitor Centre. On request the staff will show movies of the natural history of the area and the wild creatures who live there. A gift shop at the Visitor Centre sells nature books, posters, bird feeders, bird houses, music, toys and jewellery. Proceeds help to support the centre.

BLUE (INTERMEDIATE) AND YELLOW (NOVICE)

Length: 2.5 km
Time: ¹/₂ hour
Level: Novice

Detailed Tour

From the Visitor Centre follow the trail signs for the Beaver, Fox and Grouse trails. The first part of the Beaver Trail leads along the edge of an open meadow before swinging to the right, away from the woods. At the branch for the Grouse Loop take the left fork. A short distance later, follow the signs for the 2.5-km trail, branching off to the right. Soon the 5-km and 10-km sections of the Fox Trail branch off to the left. Follow the signs for the 2.5-km trail.

The trail winds through cedar woods, past a bird-feeding station where you can stop and watch a regular parade of birds coming to and going from the feeder. Signs along the way indicate the type of tracks various animals make in the snow. If you watch closely you may see the tracks of porcupine, rabbits, snowshoe hares or even a red fox.

You leave the woods and cross another open meadow area shortly before you arrive at the Visitor Centre.

Variations

The 2.2-km Grouse Loop follows the same route as the Beaver Trail, and the terrain is much the same. It is slightly shorter than the Beaver Trail and makes a fine excursion for beginning skiers.

FOX TRAIL AND VARIATIONS

Length: 5–11 km
Time: 1–2$^1/_2$ hours
Level: Intermediate

Detailed Tour

From the trail centre the route follows an old railway right of way for a short distance, then crosses an open meadow area. The track here is double set and quite level. After about half a kilometre the Grouse Loop branches right, and after another short distance, the 2.5-km Beaver Trail also branches to the right. Keep left here and follow the signs for the 5- and 10-km trails.

After you leave the Beaver Trail, the route again joins the railway right of way for almost a kilometre of wide, straight track that drops off on both sides to the forest floor below. It is strange to be looking into the forest from halfway up the trees. On your right is a tangle of thick cedar woods. On your left is much dryer and more open young hardwood forest.

When you come to the end of the straight trail, the 5-km trail branches right. There is a trail map here, and a sign warning that you should allow 2 hours to do the 10-km trail. Believe it! There are no significant shortcuts available, so don't start this section too late in the day.

Immediately past the 5-km branch the route turns sharply left into the hardwood forest. After a short uphill loop you begin climbing directly up the side of the valley. From here you begin to catch glimpses through the trees of the view over the valley. It gets better and better as you go on. A snowmobile track crosses the trail on the steepest part of the climb, just before you break out of the woods onto an open meadow area.

As you climb clear of the trees the view begins to open up behind you, where the trail turns right. The entire Wye Valley is spread out like a map before you. The town of Midland is buried in the fold of the hills on the far side of the valley. A short distance along the ridge you will see the back of a house on your left. I think that the best of the view is right here, just before the trail re-enters the forest. Be careful of frostbite on blustery days along this section.

The route through the forest continues along the top of the ridge. The drop to the valley floor on your right is steep, and you may begin to wonder how you will get down, particularly if the trails are icy. If you continue along the ridge, you come to the Foxtail Loop, which will take you down across the side of the ridge in a gentle descent. Before you get to the Foxtail you pass three shortcuts that descend the ridge in a short steep run directly down the hillside. These are the Otter Slide, the Marten Run and the Hare Cutoff. Each of these moderately difficult descents should be approached with some caution.

Once down the hill you continue through the hardwood forest until you cross the snowmobile track again. Just beyond the track there is a sharp right-hand turn on a gentle downhill slope, then the route descends easily into dense cedar woods. The woods are crisscrossed with the tracks of rabbits and snowshoe hares. You will also see signs of porcupines, where the bark is freshly stripped from the trees. From here the path is

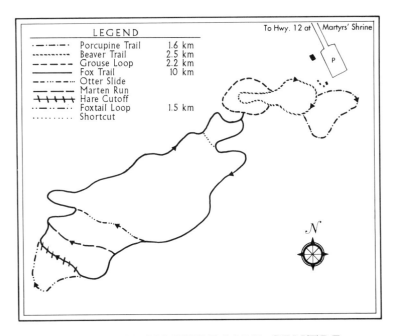

WYE MARSH WILDLIFE CENTRE

sheltered by the trees, and winds through thick bush, eventually joining the 5-km cutoff.

The route back to the Visitor Centre is easy. It passes a bird-feeding station and rejoins the Beaver Trail for the final short ski through scattered trees and open marsh meadow.

Cautions

There is an exposed area at the top of the ridge overlooking the valley. In times of severe cold and blowing snow, this is a very uncomfortable place indeed; be aware of the danger of frostbite.

Variations

The 5-km loop breaks away from this trail before it begins climbing out of the valley. This makes a fine loop that will take about an hour to ski, and offers no difficulty to intermediate or even novice skiers.

The three shortcuts at the end of the Fox Run, mentioned above, offer the most challenging sections of trail at Wye Marsh. You should attempt these only if you can comfortably control your skis on a steep pitch.

PORCUPINE

Length: 1.6 km
Time: $^1/_4$ hour
Level: Intermediate

Detailed Tour

From the start of the trails, take the left fork and follow the sign of the porcupine. The trail crosses an open meadow area and soon begins a gentle climb and swings to the right up the hill, entering a region of mixed cedar and hardwood forest.

Shortly after you enter the forest, the trail again swings left and begins a long, gradual descent. There are no turns or steep pitches here and the trail soon comes out into the open again, where it joins up with the other trails. Be prepared to stop at the trail junction. Turn to the right for the short run back to the trail centre.

Cautions

Be prepared to stop quickly where this trail intersects the Beaver and Fox trails. If you don't, you will carry on across the trails and over the edge of the old railway embankment.

Haliburton Highlands Lodge-to-Lodge Skiing

There is another aspect of cross-country skiing in Ontario that you may want to consider. Just beyond a day trip away from Toronto you can explore the Haliburton Highlands and a world of skiing in the European tradition.

Haliburton skiing requires at least a weekend, or better yet, a week, to devote to exploring new trails and new resorts and dining facilities. If you have the time and the skills, you can try lodge-to-lodge skiing. In Haliburton, fifteen ski resorts share access to an extensive trail network of about 150 km of groomed and set trails. For the 1993/94 season there were eight resorts involved in the formal lodge-to-lodge program.

The concept is simple. Go to a ski lodge, enjoy fine cuisine and all of the comforts you can imagine, such as saunas and whirlpools, and the next day ski on all new trails, never retracing your steps. Enjoy the services of a guide and have lunch on the trail. That evening, repeat the process at a different lodge. Your luggage will have been brought ahead for you and will be waiting at the next lodge.

The program is designed for the competent skier who can ski 10 to 25 km in a day without difficulty. Trails here are generally more challenging than they are at the ski areas farther south. If you are up to it and enjoy the winter outdoors, this area can give you a truly memorable ski vacation, still only a few hours' drive from home.

Location

The Haliburton Highlands ski area is located between Minden and Haliburton, about 250 km and 3 hours away from Toronto. Take Highway 404 north from Toronto, and at Newmarket go east to Highway 48. Travel 48 north and then east to Coboconk; at Coboconk take Highway 35 north to Minden. From Minden follow Highway 121 or Highway 35, depending on which resort you are headed for.

Haliburton Nordic Trails Association
P.O. Box 670
Haliburton, Ontario
K0M 1S0

Topography

The Haliburton Highlands are part of the Canadian Shield. This is an area of rugged granite outcroppings, steep hills and valleys, lakes and forests. The ski trails here seem to go on and on forever, always twisting and turning, climbing and descending through endless forests.

In all of the areas I have skied in Southern Ontario I have not found any series of trails that can rival the Haliburton trails for beauty, challenge and diversity.

Trail Map

The trail map for the linked trail system in Haliburton is quite good, and the trails are well marked with numbered signposts at all strategic locations. The map is a large foldout one with a lot of detail. On the main part of the trails the scale can be deceptive; what looks like a short distance on the map may take several hours to cover on skis.

Facilities

The main attraction here is, of course, the trails. The 154-km trail system is maintained by the Haliburton Nordic Trails Association. This is a mainly volunteer organization that grooms the trails during the winter, and maintains them during the summer, clearing brush and logs as necessary. The trails are all power groomed and track set, usually with a single-set track and a skating lane. There are several warm-up huts located on the trails, with stoves and firewood provided.

The trails are patrolled by volunteers who check for skiers needing assistance, and for anyone out there without a valid trail pass. It does cost a lot to maintain an extensive trail area like this, and most of the money comes from trail passes, so patrollers are not sympathetic when they find cheaters. They will sell you a pass right on the spot, and they get to keep half of the fees they collect on the trails, which tends to make them quite keen. The cost is only $9 per day, or $7 for a half-day pass.

The trails on this system are much more challenging than those found farther south. An intermediate trail is the equivalent of an advanced or expert trail elsewhere. Even the novice trails on some of the shorter loops have hills and steep descents.

The first afternoon I skied in Haliburton I had only a short time available, so I left from Wigamog Inn to do a short 5-km loop to Pinestone and back. My host had mentioned Heart Attack Hill, which is also known as Suicide Hill if you are descending it. As you can guess, I let my speed build up a bit too much on Suicide Hill and did a spectacular wipeout. And this was the novice run! Well, the next day I had a delightful time on the trails and I did some of the expert runs with no great problems, but never again will I say, "This is only a novice run, so I can relax."

Lodge-to-lodge skiing is very popular in Europe and is catching on in North America. Haliburton has an excellent climate and snow conditions for cross-country skiing and has the greatest concentration of linked cross-country ski resorts in Canada. It is no wonder this aspect of the sport is growing very quickly.

There are a number of Lodge-to-Lodge packages offered each year, in two-, three- or five-day excursions. The actual route of each tour will vary depending on the abilities and ambitions of the skiers on the tour. In some cases the lodges may only be a few kilometres apart, but your guide can take you on as long a tour as you wish.

During the 1993/94 season the following resorts were taking part in the lodge-to-lodge program.

Deer Lodge

Deer Lodge is a medium-sized family run resort that has a lot of repeat business. The staff concentrate on providing their guests with the best hospitality and service. The lounge boasts the largest granite fireplace I have ever seen, reputedly the largest in Canada. This is a place where it is easy to feel right at home almost as soon as you walk in. Guests stay in their own individual cabins.

Hart Resort

Hart Resort is on Highway 35, overlooking the falls at the lower end of Twelve Mile Lake. The resort offers a variety of accommodation options ranging from conventional rooms to studio suites and apartments with fireplaces and kitchenettes.

Heather Lodge

Heather Lodge, also located on Twelve Mile Lake, is the smallest of the resorts on the lodge-to-lodge program. When you sit down in front of the fireplace in the main lounge you feel as if you are in your own living room. In the evening you can chat with new friends, or perhaps get up a game of bridge. Hosts Bob and Heather Cairns are always happy to spend time with their guests, and Bob is an expert skier who can share his knowledge of the trails with you.

Lakeview Motel

Lakeview Motel is a basic, comfortable, family-oriented motel offering an economical place to stay while skiing in Haliburton. After a day on the trails, you can come into the lounge, pat the cat who spends most of his winters soaking up the heat under the wood stove, and have a cup of tea with your hosts, John and Ennis Felts.

Except for the lodge-to-lodge program, Lakeview does not normally offer dinner, but breakfast is always available, whenever you want it. There is a good choice of restaurants only a few minutes' drive down the road, so there is no problem finding someplace to dine. Nearby Glebe Park, just north of

Haliburton Village, offers lighted trails for night skiing, all included in the cost of your daily trail pass.

Locarno

Locarno is a medium-sized resort with excellent facilities. It appeals mostly to couples who want to avoid the noise and hustle of more crowded places. The individual chalets, each with a fireplace and whirlpool bath, offer a dandy place for a romantic weekend with few distractions. The dining room and lounge, both done in old knotty pine, are bright comfortable rooms with a wonderful view over Lake Kashawigamog.

Maple Sands

Maple Sands, located on Maple Lake, is at the north end of the trail system. This small, rustic resort has ten rooms and six individual chalets. It is a challenging expedition to ski to Maple Sands, but once you are there you will find the place informal and relaxing. There are about 8 km of trails maintained by Maple Sands on their own property. There is also a real maple bush on the property with a maple syrup shack that is due to resume operation in the spring of 1995.

Pinestone Inn

Pinestone Inn is a new, modern hotel and convention centre offering all of the amenities to be found in the best resorts anywhere. Here you will find all the comforts you could wish for, including an excellent pool and hot tub. The dining room is first rate, and there is regular entertainment in the lounge. The pro shop offers a full range of equipment for sale or rent.

Wigamog Inn

Wigamog is a "Country Casual Inn," an old family-owned resort dating from the early 1900s. Wigamog has found a near perfect compromise between the efficiency of a modern facility and the rustic charm of an old establishment filled with the memories of generations of owners and guests.

Every morning during breakfast, the ski pro, Blake, comes through the dining room to check on who is skiing, offering advice on current trail conditions and helping to make sure that everyone has the best ski outing possible.

Dining at the Wigamog is a mixture of quiet elegance and good times as the staff organize the evening's events. For relaxing after a day on the trails, the hot tub and sauna are always available and usually not crowded.

❄   ❄   ❄   ❄   ❄

If the idea of skiing 10 to 25 km a day over intermediate and advanced trails appeals to you, then you are sure to enjoy a lodge-to-lodge skiing holiday in Haliburton.